The
Bible
Unmasked

by Joseph Lewis

Author of
"The Tyranny of God,"
"Lincoln the Freethinker,"
"Jefferson the Freethinker," etc.

"

This book has been published by:

Contact: sales@nuvisionpublications.com
URL: http://www.nuvisionpublications.com

Publishing Date: 2007

ISBN# 1-59547-945-7

Please see my website for several books created for
education, research and entertainment.

Specializing in rare, out-of-print books still in demand.

The first edition of The Bible Unmasked consists of 250 copies, printed on special paper, with gold top pages, and bound in limp leather with title stamped in gold. Each copy is numbered and autographed by the author. This is the first general edition.

Dedication

This book is dedicated in all seriousness to rabbis, priests and ministers, in the hole that it may bring them to realize the fraud they are perpetrating by preaching the Bible as the Word of God, and as a moral ant intellectual guide for or the human race.

-- *Joseph Lewis.*

"Any system of religion that has anything in it that shocks the mind of a child, cannot be a true system."

-- *Thomas Paine.*

By this time the whole world should know that the real Bible has not yet been written, but is being written, and that it will never be finished until the race begins its downward march, or ceases to exist."

"The real Bible is not the work of inspired men, nor prophets nor apostles, nor evangelists, nor of Christs. Every man who finds a fact adds, as it were, a word to this great book. It is not attested by prophecy, by miracles or signs. It makes no appeal to faith, to ignorance, to credulity or fear. It has no punishment for unbelief, and no reward for hypocrisy. It appeals to man in the name of demonstration. It has nothing to conceal. It has no fear of being read, of being contradicted, of being investigated and understood. It does not pretend to be holy or sacred; it simply claims to be true. It challenges the scrutiny of all, and implores every reader to verify every line for himself. It is incapable of being blasphemed. This book appeals to all the surroundings of man. Each thing that exists testifies to its perfection. The earth, with its heart of fire and crowns of snow; with its forests and plains, its rocks and seas; with its every wave and cloud; with its every leaf and bud and flower, confirms its every word, and the solemn stars, shining in the infinite abysses, are the eternal witnesses of its truth."

-- *Robert G. Ingersoll.*

Table of Contents

Introduction.

"The duty of a philosopher is clear.
He must take every pain to ascertain the truth;
and, having arrived at a conclusion,
he should noise it abroad far and wide,
utterly regardless of what opinions he shocks."

-- Henry Thomas Buckle.

In taking as my subject for this book the question of the morality, or rather the immorality of the Bible, I realize at once the importance and delicacy of the subject. This is true, because what is immoral in one age and time, may at some other time, be considered moral, and what we to-day may consider moral and acceptable, may at some future date be condemned as being immoral.

There is in reality no absolute standard by which we may judge; and in the final analysis our guide in moral affairs should be that which gives to the individual the greatest possible happiness, and which at the same time will inflict no harm upon another individual. Even under this rule there may be instances where a higher and more altruistic principle would be necessary to insure the best interest of the community and to society at large.

Therefore, the subject that I have chosen for my book is as delicate as it is serious, as there is always the possibility of saying something that may be entirely at variance with the conceptions of some of us regarding morality and its phases.

I think I can appropriately quote the poet Moore in his definition of morality, when he says:

"I find the doctors and sages
Have differed in all climes and ages,
And two in fifty scarce agree
On what is pure morality."

The utmost discretion must also be used in such a discussion to avoid any injustice to the individual to the preference of society, and with scrupulous integrity the same rule must be applied to society in its relationship to the individual. Science must formulate the principle of a moral guide. We must disregard all past conventions, except to learn from their shortcomings, so as better to avoid similar pitfalls in the future. We must start anew, so to speak, for the rules and guides which now govern our conduct have been proven false and utterly inadequate for the needs of modern existence.

We are still using for our guide, rules which are as obsolete as a belief in the flatness of the earth.

A new order of morality must be ushered in and it must of necessity be just as revolutionary and just as beneficial to the human race as were the scientific discoveries of the eighteenth and nineteenth centuries, which upset all previous conventions and calculations and started mankind upon a career of unparalleled progress.

We must begin the other way round, and instead of our acts being performed solely for divine approbation, we must do our utmost for the benefit of the individual, which in the last analysis is also for the best interest of society. It will be man's relation to man that will become the holy thing. Humanity and not God will be our chief concern. Our acts will not be performed for the purpose of future rewards, but rather for present benefits.

Again, the delicacy of my subject becomes apparent from the fact that certain words and expressions must be used that may shock the sensibilities of certain persons. But this I promise, that any words I may use in this book which may offend or shock any one who reads will not be words or expressions I have purposely selected to designate a character or to express a situation, but will be words and expressions which I have found in the stories as recorded in the Bible.

Let me repeat: if there are words and expressions used which are unfit for refined conversation, these words and expressions will be taken from the Bible which contains the stories I have selected as being, in the light of our present knowledge and progress, immoral, offensive and obscene.

And if you are not acquainted with the words, language, and expressions of the Bible, I ask you kindly to close this book; do not read it unless you want to learn the truth about the Bible. I am not concerned with the truth or falsity of the stories from which I shall quote, but with the fact that these stories are in the Bible and that the Bible is considered holy and sacred -- a divinely inspired book. Were it not for this fact my labor would be unnecessary, and I would not engage myself in it.

I am not writing this treatise as a member of any particular creed, for I do not belong to any. I am writing it as a member of the human family, without regard to race or religion, and for the benefit of all mankind.

The Bible has for many ages been considered as the Holy Word of an Ever-Existing God, and no one has been permitted to question its truth in any respect. It has ruled as the supreme authority in every line of thought; in every field of endeavor, and in every human relationship. At one time, to refuse to be bound by its precepts meant death by the most horrible means that perverted minds could inflict upon a human being. In fact, to doubt the divine origin of the Bible was the most flagrant of crimes.

Erasmus declared that heresy was a greater crime than impurity of life. That Christianity cared more for blind faith than uprightness of living is attested only too well by the pages of history. And the charge that religion and morals are synonymous terms is either stupidity or deliberate fraud. By its very precepts, by its expounders, and by its professors, religion has been proven to be the very antithesis of morality.

The first great step in the emancipation of the minds of the people from the ignorance and superstition of the Bible came about when Galileo put a crude telescope to the sky and removed our earth from the center of the universe, as it was supposed to be, to the tiny insignificant speck in a mighty realm of space, that it actually is. The great conflict between knowledge and superstition began when Astronomy was put upon a scientific basis.

To state briefly this conflict, is to say that the Science of Astronomy has no use for the knowledge, if you can call it such, of the Bible. We all are acquainted with the fact that from the Bible the people became convinced that the earth was the center of the universe, and for centuries no one dared make an attempt to prove the contrary. Oh yes, there were some, but Bruno's heroic statue in Rome bespeaks only too eloquently the price that was paid for matching scientific and philosophic deductions against bigotry and God's Word.

We know that from the Bible ignorant people were convinced that God was sitting in the clouds and for that reason they lifted their hands and raised their voices in appeals for help. Astronomy pointed a telescope to the spot where God was supposed to be and found no such character there. If upon the invention of the telescope God moved to a different abode, he left no trace of his former occupancy. Astronomers, using the most powerful telescopes, telescopes that can scan the universe for millions of miles, testify they can find no trace of such a being, and that God must be some crafty creature to have made his getaway under the circumstances. For there are stars within the domain of man's exploration whose light-rays require thousands of years to reach us, and if God is beyond the region of these stars he is certainly useless to us, because in less time than would be required for him to come to our assistance the human race might be no more.

But God for the moment is not our subject; neither is prayer, nor the Science of Astronomy. We are concerned for the moment with the fact only that the Science of Astronomy, which should find some benefit in the Bible, since it is supposed to deal with the region of space in which Astronomy is interested, rejects that book completely, by saying: the

Bible may be perfectly satisfactory as a moral guide, but it contains nothing of value to Astronomy.

The Geologists, the Naturalists, the Zoologists, the Botanists, the Biologists, the Physicists, the Physiologists and in fact all the Scientists are perfectly willing you should use the Bible as a moral guide, so long as you do not insist that they accept it as a standard of truth in their respective spheres. They all come to the same conclusion, that the Bible does not contain a solitary scientific truth.

Let us now examine and discover for ourselves whether the moralist has any use for the Bible, a book that is not only supposed to contain all the knowledge of the world, but that has been held over the heads of the people and sacredly worshipped for so many hundreds of years. I will not dwell upon, nor go into the details of the gross immorality that the Bible has caused; but rather I will discuss those phases of morality which deal with the social or sexual relation of man to society, such as rape, adultery, licentiousness, unfaithfulness and things universally condemned as being opprobrious. The evidence from the Bible itself will destroy its value as a moral guide.

It is a common experience to come in contact with persons who tell me that if the Bible has stood the test for so many years it is good enough for them. I reply that slavery stood the test as an existing institution for a longer period than the Bible has been revered, and yet chattel slavery does not exist to-day. Even so great a mind as Aristotle said that without slavery civilization could not exist. And since the physical slave has been emancipated, let us break the spell of the Bible and its attendant enslaving superstition and liberate completely the mind of man. Freedom of the mind is surely equal in importance to freedom of the body.

And as I am asked from time to time similar questions as to why the Bible still persists, I of course give different instances of long-established standards that are no longer followed by the progressive world. History records many "sacred" books that were once held in awe and reverence, but which are now looked upon as ancient curiosities. The Bible is but another of these "sacred" volumes and is unfortunately far inferior to most of them in moral precepts.

The insane are no longer tortured. We now treat them as mentally diseased. Witchcraft, once so commonly prevalent, is now known to have been religious superstition carried to its ultimate end. Religious mania triumphant! John Wesley spoke the truth when he said, "The giving up of witchcraft is, in effect, the giving up of the Bible." At one time the belief was prevalent and religiously maintained that onions caused cancer; that beads could cure scarlet fever, and that to shave the upper lip was to impare your eyesight!

For ages the adage "Spare the rod and spoil the child" prevailed in the treatment of children. Tender tots were unmercifully beaten by cruel parents. The wide leather strap was an essential part of the household. If there were no family skeleton in the closet. you would be sure to find the child-beating strap there. "If we did not beat the child and put 'fear' into him, how else were we to make him 'good' and have 'respect for his elders'?" was the argument that triumphantly maintained this brutal system. In the days gone by, and I am not so sure that they have passed, the religious-minded could not conceive of any other method of correction. To spare the rod and spoil the child was a sacrilege and an unpardonable act in the sight of God.

Part and parcel with this method went the fear implanted in the imagination of the child by the weird and frightful tales of the "bogey man" and the terrifying ghosts. This fear implanted in the mind of a child is just as poisonous as the venom of a snake. To-day psychology has corrected this brutal and barbarous method in connection with the training of children. Intelligence and its application were the solution, and no greater triumph has been achieved by science than has been accomplished in the realm of child training. And although there are many still tainted with the Biblical notion of physical punishment in the treatment of children, no truly civilized man or woman to-day would use such a heinous method.

And yet in the New York Times for August 22, 1925, the Reverend R. M. Bradner, assistant minister, St. George's Church, New York City, made a plea to go back to this barbarous custom in the treatment of children.

And just as the child does not need something to put fear into him as a corrective, neither do adults need the "fear of something" to keep them good.

Fear, "fear of God" or any other fear, is a negative and destructive force no matter how it is applied. Courage is the watchword and intelligence the key to proper conduct. In the larger realm of human misconduct, punishment as a corrective to fit the crime is an altogether different principle from fear as a deterrent with the subsequent "forgiveness" after the act without the slightest understanding of wrongdoing or of rectification.

The knowledge of the right and the mental strength to follow that right is the ultimate end and goal of education. To commit your crime, "to confess your sins and be absolved of the deed," may be a satisfactory religious doctrine, but it is inimical to justice and human welfare.

I know a man who used to beat his child. The strap was used with much force and vigor without the slightest feeling of compunction. And when I told him he was committing a grave wrong in beating his child he looked at me in blank amazement. I had actually astounded him. He was stunned and speechless. He thought that the beating of his child was as right and as essential as the rising and the setting of the sun and as natural as that night should follow day. His father beat him and no doubt his father was beaten by his paternal ancestor and so it was established beyond the peradventure of a doubt that the corporal punishment of children was not only the only possible method, but was a parent's inalienable and unforfeitable right.

I analyzed his case and told him to make a "pal" and confidant of his boy. I told him he could accomplish much more by kindness and with love in a spirit of understanding than by any other method. Although his face still wore that amazed and stunned look, he promised to try my suggestions; and now after a lapse of nearly three years he boasts of never having struck his child during that period and confesses he owes me a debt that he can never repay. And yet -- and this is the humorous part -- he still looks upon my "infidel" opinions as being something beyond the realm of understanding, despite the fact it was an "infidel" who brought the light of understanding to his "enlightened" Christian mind. History proves that it has invariably been the infidels who have been the humanitarians, the torchbearers, the pathfinders not only of progress but also of human understanding, of love and of sympathy. And if Progress is the aim of mankind, if Liberty is its goal, and Freedom its destiny, then the Bible as a sacred book must go, religion as superstition must cease, and the church as an institution must be abandoned.

Are not the words of Professor Garrett P. Serviss, worth quoting here?

"The only real road to settled peace is that of science; politics will never hit it, nor dogmatic religion either. Science is, in its very nature, universal. It interests all civilized nations alike. It has no favorites, and no preferred views. Its aim is absolutely single, viz, the uncovering of the truth. Knowledge is power -- not partial but complete power, which cannot make war upon itself.

"Mankind has tried the other two roads to peace -- the road of political jealousy and the road of religious bigotry -- and found them both equally misleading. Perhaps it will now try the third, the road of scientific truth, the only road on which the passenger is not deceived -- like a skittish horse with blinders. Science does not, ostrich-like, bury its head amidst perils and difficulties. It tries to see everything exactly as everything is."

Abundant evidence and prison statistics are available to prove the prevalence of the moral and ethical misdeeds of the religious elect. Reference to them is constantly found in the daily papers.

Let us, as a matter of comparison, assume that Freethinkers were guilty of the same crimes as religious believers; the charge would be made that it was their infidel" books, teachings and examples that were responsible for their criminal acts; and there would be a hue and cry over the length and breadth of this land to suppress and destroy all "infidel" literature. We would never hear the end of the "direful influence" such teachings would have upon the minds of people.

If we apply this rule to Freethinkers, let us use the same measurement to religious believers and determine whether or not their books, teachings and examples are responsible for their crimes. Let us be honest. Let us be fair.

What would be said if a prominent Freethinker were to use the words that were so boldly and defiantly uttered by Father Phelan in the "Western Watchman" of June 27, 1913:

"Tell us we are Catholics first and Americans or Englishmen afterwards; of course we are. Tell us, in the conflict between the church and the civil government we take the side of the church; of course we do. Why, if the government of the United States were at war with the church, we would say tomorrow, To hell with the government of the United States; and if the church and all the governments of the world were at war, we would say, To hell with all the governments of the world. Why is it that in this country, where we have only seven percent of the population, the Catholic church is so much feared? She is loved by all her children and feared by everybody. Why is it that the Pope has such tremendous power? Why, the Pope is the ruler of the world. All the emperors, all the kings, all the princes, all the presidents of the world, are as these altar boys of mine. The Pope is the ruler of the world.[1]"

As I said before, no one can claim absolute law in the matter of morality, but there are some things repugnant to all of us and which will not be tolerated in the relationship of man to man. These repugnant acts are so self-evident that everywhere, in no matter what strata of society they exist, they are met with condemnation and censure.

The question of morals; the question of sex; the question of the relation of the individual to society, and of the relation of society to the individual, are all questions of such tremendous importance that each one, to be discussed properly, would require a book for itself. But this much we know: those who have the broadest and most liberal attitude upon these questions generally live the highest and most upright lives. And those who have set dogmatic rules and seek to impose them as guidance for others, are often the ones who lead the most questionable lives.

If it has taken so many centuries to convince the people of simple truths in the scientific realm, one can realize how difficult it will be to

---

[1] Quoted from Upton Sinclair's "Profits of Religion," page 119.

bring the people's minds out of the mass of misinterpretation and ignorance that has so long befogged them in the sphere of morality, where the scientific base, as in many other fields, is not so apparent.

To the Puritans, it was not only breaking a moral law, but also a disgrace to kiss one's wife on Sunday. A breach was also established, for which a penalty was exacted, if one were to kiss even his child on this "sacred day." To be seen on the streets on Sunday, except to "walk reverently to and from Church," was so flagrant a violation of the moral code that the perpetrator paid the penalty by a public ducking!

The mockery of it all! It was immoral for any one to be seen upon the public streets on Sunday, except on his way to church, to listen to a preacher "expounding" and "explaining" some of the incongruities, stupidities and immoralities of the Bible!

But this religious insanity did not exist only among the Puritans. It is found wherever Biblical teaching takes precedence over reason and intelligence. It is the inevitable consequence of permitting "instruments of God" and "divinely inspired men" to make our laws and govern our affairs. It reaches its highest form whenever this vile superstition rules the land, as was the case in the days of the Spanish Inquisition.

In Scotland, where the Scotch Presbyterian long held sway, it was a sin for any one to hold market on Saturday or Monday because both days were near Sunday. It was also sinful to go from one town to another, however pressing the need. It was a sin to visit a friend, or water the garden, or to shave, or to walk in the meadows, or to sit in the doorway to enjoy the weather, or even to sleep on the "Lord's Day." Bathing, being pleasant and wholesome, was a particularly grievous offense and therefore was prohibited on Sunday. In fact, it was doubtful whether public bathing was lawful for a Christian at any time. To be clean was considered a sacrilege; and to enjoy one's repast was proof of a sinful nature. But to continue to repeat these hallucinations would be to fill an entire volume. These fanatics went so far as to admonish the people, that on Sundays in particular they should never think of benefiting others; and on that day it was even sinful to save a vessel in distress; and that it was a proof of religion -- for it was God's will -- to let the ship sink and the crew perish.[2]

I suppose they received the inspiration for their acts from the sabbath of the Jews, who on Saturdays in particular and on sacred days in general, are not "allowed" to perform labor of any kind. What a tragedy it is to be under such a fearful spell of superstition!

To many people even to-day, it is highly immoral for a woman too expose her leg beyond a certain point. And only recently we read an account of a Catholic priest who refused to "bless" his congregation

---

[3] Buckle, "History of Civilization in England," vol. III, pages 265 to 276.

because a woman, kneeling in front of him, wore a waist which, when she bent over for "blessing," did not cover the shapeliness of her bosom.

What right the priest had to look at the woman's bosom so exposed I will not discuss. For the life of me, I cannot see what the unintentional exposure of a woman's bosom, particularly to a priest, has to do with blessings from a direct messenger of God. And the New York Times of August 11, 1924, in a cable from Bergamo, Italy, quotes the Mgr. Marelli, Bishop of Bergamo, on women who "lewdly expose their nudity," as saying, "Women must enter church decently dressed, with head and breast covered, without décolleté and with arms covered. Their gowns must be sufficiently long and without indecent transparencies."

Bishop Marelli has also ordered nuns in monasteries who conduct laundries to refuse to wash any articles of clothing which are "indicative of indecency."

If a priest or any one else has any objection to the form, dress or acts of any one as being immoral, what must we say when we examine the Bible in our search for a moral guide?

If the Bible contained real knowledge, if it were a book that made an endeavor to uplift the world and bring us above the level from which man began his existence, we would revere its writers and keep its principles as our guide with a sacredness and devotion justly deserved.

If the Bible contained scientific knowledge that the world is actually crying for to-day, but which the bigoted and superstitious are doing their utmost to retard, what a glorious difference this book would have made upon the civilization of man!

If the Bible instructed man, or at least made an effort to enlighten him, in the intimate relations of life, which when understood and properly consummated, produce the highest and noblest in man, but when viciously indulged in, become the most degraded and perverted practice, what a joy there would be in devoting our lives to the practice and dissemination of its precepts and principles!

How often do we look back over our path of life and bemoan our mistakes; and every one knows that the mistakes that most sharply penetrate our consciousness are the ones made in the sexual realm. We know the sorrows caused by the ignorance of the laws of sex, and we know also that this ignorance multiplies a hundredfold the misery found in the married state. We are also thoroughly familiar with the fact that this ignorance is the primary cause of marital unhappiness and eventually leads to the divorce court.

It has been conservatively estimated that during the past twenty years there have been nearly two million divorces in the United States alone. What poignant disillusionment is suffered by the parties of a married union that causes their love to turn to bitterness and hatred and impels them to seek freedom from each other! What torment and misery do they suffer before they have the courage to permit the sneering public to gossip about their private lives!

Statistics are not always accurate. They do not always reveal the true conditions. It is invariably true that regardless of the number, percentage or proportion of unhappy couples that bring their cases to public light, there are a greater number that suppress their feelings, bear their sorrow and live their lives in abject horror because they do not possess the courage to demand a public rectification of their mistakes. It is knowledge, knowledge, KNOWLEDGE that the world needs, and if the Bible contained that knowledge nine-tenths of the misery that is now suffered by the people would be unknown, and instead a relationship productive of some benefit and pleasure would be the result. Happiness would be exchanged for misery and smiles and laughter would be the rule and not the exception.

What must we say when books, the results of years of careful study and investigation, containing the sexual truth and enlightenment that are so sadly needed by the people, are suppressed, and the Bible is not only circulated freely, but actually forced upon the people by law!

I could mention three books, which, were they issued with each marriage license, would obliterate ninety-five per cent of the now prevailing unhappiness, due to the ignorance of the laws of sex, and would usher in a new order and a new era of marital understanding and happiness. But it is my purpose here to tell you only about the Bible. And when you become fully acquainted with the Bible and what it contains you will no longer wonder why the intellectual world rejects it completely.

It has become a common expression and axiom, that only those believe the Bible who have not read it. And when I say they believe it, I mean that they are under the impression that the book contains the most exalted and noblest rules by which life should be governed. But what a fearful mistake that is! The Bible is the contrary in its moral guidance as it is in any other field of thought.

We can forgive the Bible its mistakes in the scientific fields, but we cannot condone its coarseness and vulgarity in the moral sphere, where it is now being foisted upon us. Whipped and beaten by every other line of thought the Bible is now being proposed as the paragon of moral teachings.

The question of religious liberty has been settled and nearly all the governments of the world have made provisions and protection for it. It behooves us, then, to tell the real truth about the Bible and once and for all settle the bitter differences that have been the cause of so much dissension and strife throughout the world. As soon as the people become acquainted with the fact that the Bible is an unworthy book, when that false halo of sanctity has been removed, one of the heaviest burdens will have been lifted from the minds of the world, and resources amounting to wealth incalculable will be released for the common good.

Therefore it is our duty to expose the Bible. And although there have been others who have devoted their lives and fortunes in enlightening the people, their efforts have been unable to accomplish all. We must continue to tell the truth about the Bible. We must continue to enlighten the people. We must never fail to do our part. And if, after the true facts are known, there are some who still insist the Bible is good enough for them, they are welcome to it. They are entitled to their "faith in filth!"[3] and I for one will fight that they may always possess the right and liberty to be fully protected in their belief.

The Bible is a collection of miscellaneous and disconnected stories that have been preserved, and their original purpose was no more to masquerade as being "inspired" than any of the lascivious stories of Balzac.

The education of mankind cannot really begin until the minds of men have been uneducated from the great mass of superstition and falsehood that has been inculcated in them from the Bible. History proves the truth of Buckle's statement that, "Every great reform which has been effected has consisted, not in doing something new, but in undoing something old."

And how any enlightened country, particularly a republic, can tolerate the Bible in its governmental activities is a situation difficult to understand, unless the officials in power are not acquainted with the history of progress and are utterly ignorant of the price of Liberty.

Thomas Jefferson has truthfully said, "In every country and in every age the priest has been hostile to liberty; he is always in alliance with the despot, abetting his abuses in return for protection to his own."

And who can deny the truth of Buckle's statement: "A careful study of religious toleration will show that in every Christian country where it has been adopted, it has been forced upon the clergy by the authority of the secular classes."

The infamous doctrine of monarchy is not only upheld, but is supposed to carry divine right, by Biblical testimony. The greatest fight in the emancipation of the negro slave was to overcome the sanction of this terrible institution by the numerous texts in the Bible which maintained that slavery was prescribed by God. It is common history

---

[3] In using the word "filth" in reference to the Biblical narratives, I wish it understood that its use is intended to reflect the same thought that would be expressed by the religious-minded in judging the literature of sex as found in books other than the Bible.

that the slave-holder's staunchest support, North and South, was that arm of the Bible known as the Christian Church. I want to avoid any discussion that does not directly touch upon the subject of this book and must therefore check myself upon any further points of this nature, leaving them for another opportunity. Indeed, volumes have been written upon this phase of Biblical influence. But let us get back to its moral side.

In the Bible will be found the most degrading word, applicable to woman, in the language of the human race. Mind you! It is mentioned not in the sense that the life the word signifies should be avoided as abhorrent, but it is mentioned in connection with men and women of the Bible after whom fond parents consider it a great honor to name their sons and daughters. I am going to mention this word in the course of this book, as I am sure that if the people were acquainted with what the Bible actually contains they would discard it completely as being utterly unfit for cultural reading.

As a piece of fiction, the Bible ranks, when truthfully weighed, far beneath the great entrancing stories of the French novelists. By comparison with the celebrated masterpieces of erotic composition, the Bible is lacking in that charm and delicacy of expression and is utterly void in its moral conclusion, which so distinguishes this kind of literature. Standards and appreciations are, in a great measure, a matter of personal preference and opinion, and I will leave, therefore, after you have read this book, the question of the Bible's worth to your own judgment.

There have been many instances when Robert G. Ingersoll offered one hundred dollars in gold to any preacher who would read certain parts of the Bible to his congregation, but so far as I know no clergyman ever came forward to claim the money. There is a saying to the effect that "what cannot be spoken, may be sung," so in the course of this book I will mention some of those parts to you.

As long as the Bible is permitted to be read in the home, and the government sanctions it by permitting it to be sent through the mail, I do not think I will trespass much upon indiscretion when I quote from its chapters.

I wish this borne in mind: it is not what I say about the stories in the Bible that makes them so offensive; it is the stories themselves, steeped in all the sordidness of vulgarity, that makes them so shocking and harmful. It is the example of the stories that we are concerned with. They lack the moral viewpoint we want to instill and the power to elevate and uplift. It is what the Bible does not tell in its relation to morality that is of so much importance.

I sincerely trust that anyone who reads this book will never again abuse the world "Holy" in referring to the Bible. Never again should the word "good" be applied to the Bible, which has been found to be so distinctly bad and vulgar. As to making mention that it is divine, all I can say is: I have only sympathy for the deluded, the superstitious and the insane. I am in perfect accord with Havelock Ellis, who claims that were the treatment of the insane in early Biblical times on the same scientific plane that it is to-day, the Bible would never have been written.

It is a conspicious fact that the Bible not only does not contain a moral guide, but it does not contain even the words "moral" and "morality."

Surely its pages bespeak the reason why. The writers of the Bible had little conception of what was moral, or right; and as to the meaning and understanding of morality they were pitifully ignorant. The writers of the Bible had slight concern for the principles of morality. They were more concerned with rape, murder. robbery, slavery, licentiousness, brutal ignorance and degrading superstition.

Some may think, in the reading of this book, that I have picked out the so-called immoral parts of the Bible to lower its estimation in the minds of the people.

Such a conclusion is an admission of the fact, and of the Bible's guilt!

You will be able to determine for yourself, by consulting the Bible, whether or not I am telling the truth.

The first story from the Bible that contains subject matter for my book appears just at the beginning of Biblical history, after "God" had destroyed the world and had made Noah the Commander-in-Chief of all living things. It is just after the success of the Flood that our first story begins, and let us see what a race of perfect, moral people God created, since the first lot was not satisfactory.

It is regrettable that we have no record of the history of the people God destroyed, as I believe their wickedness would have made a fine contrast to those the Lord preserved. But this is pardonable, for the story of Noah, the Ark, and the Flood is now considered, even by high church dignitaries, to have been a monstrous "fish story." It will not be necessary to turn many pages to get to the stories of the Bible, which, by reading, will bring a blush of shame to your cheeks, despite the fact that they will be taken from the book that has so long been regarded and reverenced and legally protected as the "Holy Scriptures."

Chapter I.

Abram And Sarai.[4]

The most sacred relation of life is the devotion, the integrity, and the loyalty of a man and a woman. Without this relationship, without the mutual pledge and keeping of a sacred faith with each other, there would be nothing in life to warrant its puny existence. Anything that tends to strengthen this tie of love, that makes for a more happy union and sacred trust, is a force of uplift, of advancement, of progress, and of happiness. Anything that undermines this relationship, that tends to break its bonds, that puts a commercial price upon its devotion is not only harmful, but belongs to the baser things of life which civilization abhors as a plague. For after all, when the sum total of life has been thoroughly analyzed, it is as Robert Burns would say:

"To build a happy fire-side clime for weans and wife,
Is the true pathos and sublime of human life."

For a man to betray a woman in the marital relationship is a deed of grave injustice and for a woman to betray a man in this same relationship is one of the basest of acts. And yet, we sanction the separation of a pair when their union is incompatible and makes their lives a burden instead of a source of happiness in this world of so much pain and sorrow. But if this sacred relationship is used by either party for personal gain and personal safety, or, to secure special favor or special dispensation, our condemnation for such an act is only too well known.

Still, in the Bible, there are related acts of such a character; that are not only not condemned, but the parties thereto receive the blessing and bountifulness of God.

We will proceed to relate a story of such a despicable nature. I quote Genesis, Chapter 12, Verses 11-20.

11. And it came to pass, when he was come near to enter into Egypt, that he said unto Sarai his wife, Behold now, I know that thou art a fair woman to look upon:

12. Therefore it shall come to pass, when the Egyptians shall see thee, that they shall say, This is his wife: and they will kill me, but they will save thee alive.

---

[4] The Bible used as reference in this work is the King James version, published by the American Bible Society. "Its sole object," says the printed statement of the society, "is *to encourage the wider circulation of the Holy Scriptures without note or comment.*" It also boasts of having issued over 158,000,000 volumes during its existence.

13. *Say, I pray thee, thou art my sister: that it may be well with me for thy sake; and my soul shall live because of thee.*

14. *And it came to pass, that, when Abram was come into Egypt, the Egyptians beheld the woman that she was very fair.*

15. *The princes also of Pharaoh saw her, and commended her before Pharaoh: and the woman was taken into Pharaoh's house.*

16. *And he entreated Abram well for her sake: and he had sheep, and oxen, and he asses, and menservants and maidservants, and she asses, and camels.*

17. *And the Lord plagued Pharaoh and his house with great plagues, because of Sarai, Abram's wife.*

18. *And Pharaoh called Abram, and said, What is this that thou hast done unto me? why didst thou not tell me that she was thy wife?*

19. *Why saidst thou, She is my sister? so I might have taken her to me to wife: now therefore behold thy wife, take her, and go thy way.*

20. *And Pharaoh commanded his men concerning him: and they sent him away, and his wife, and all that he had.*

Now in the character of Abram we have a man who has been extolled for centuries throughout the world as the product of the finest and best in life. Particularly one whose services in behalf of the Lord should be followed by every one. It was Abram, remember, who received the Covenant from God. And his fame is similar to that of our own George Washington, because he is considered the "Father of the Jewish People." But let me ask: Would you under the pretext of saving yourself, force your wife whom you love, to commit an act of prostitution in order that you might secure safe passage in your travels from one country to another?

Sarai's desires and rights in the matter were of no concern, as long as Abram was sure of protection and free of molestation. We cannot take into consideration, in this narrative, the childish element of God in this transaction, unless we also make him a party to the deal; a deal in which a man's wife is of so little value that he readily consented to have her submit to the embraces of other men in order that he himself might escape harm.

There is no doubt that Sarai performed her part of the bargain with full value, as Pharaoh "entreated Abram well for her sake." It seems in this pretty piece of business sagacity that our sympathies should be with Pharaoh, and our condemnation and contempt for Abram, the Lord notwithstanding to the contrary. Pharaoh distinctly tells Abram, after he has learned the truth, that if he had known that Sarai was Abram's wife, he would not have committed his adulterous act.

Pharaoh should be our model in this story instead of this gentleman whom we are pleased to call the "Father of the Jewish People." Is it from stories like this that our daughters are to receive their impressions and examples of virtue?

Is this the story that the prospective wife is to have before her as an example when she marries the man of her choice; especially, if she is a devout believer in the holiness and sacredness of every word that the Bible contains? Must she picture to herself, when in such a circumstance as related above, that her husband will surrender her to the lust of a stranger so that he may remain unharmed and unhurt? Or, rather, should she select a man as her mate, who follows the example of one who will at all times and under all circumstances protect her first and defend himself afterwards -- one who will lay down his life for her safety?

Further comment upon this story, is, I believe, unnecessary as it speaks its own foul lesson better than anything else could. But we are not finished with this model pair of the Bible, and I must give you another glimpse of their code of morals. One would think that the above story would be sufficient to make any one couple notorious, but the Bible-makers thought additional information of their intimate life would be elevating. And so I quote, Genesis, Chapter 16, Verses 1-2.

Now Sarai, Abram's wife, bare him no children: and she had a handmaid, an Egyptian, whose name was Hagar.

2. And Sarai said unto Abram, Behold now, the Lord hath restrained me from bearing: I pray thee, go in unto my maid; it may be that I may obtain children by her. And Abram hearkened to the voice of Sarai.

Rather a nice compromising situation; a particularly desirable one for a profligate husband; also a particularly liberal and obliging wife. Can you picture the situation as related above? Sarai tells Abram, "I pray thee, go in unto my maid," and the Bible assures us there was no hesitation on the part of Abram as he "hearkened to the voice of Sarai."

To-day the conditions seem to be the reverse. When a wife discovers that her husband is getting a bit too familiar with the maid, she generally consults her lawyer regarding a divorce, and quite a number of divorces have been granted where the maid has been mentioned as the corespondent. But there is more to follow and so we continue.

Genesis, Chapter 16 Verses 3-5.

3. And Sarai, Abram's wife, took Hagar her maid the Egyptian, after Abram had dwelt ten years in the land of Canaan, and gave her to her husband Abram to be his wife.

4. And he went in unto Hagar, and she conceived: and when she saw that she had conceived, her mistress was despised in her eyes.

5. And Sarai said unto Abram, My wrong be upon thee: I have given my maid into thy bosom; and when she saw that she had conceived, I was despised in her eyes: the Lord judge between me and thee.

Certainly here is a situation where an appeal to the law seems the only solution. What jealousy arises in a woman's breast under such circumstances I do not know; yet it does seem but natural that when a mistress forces her servant to co-habit with her husband, and when this cohabitation results in a pregnancy, surely the servant is justified in demanding that her mistress's husband give her all the protection that a woman in her condition deserves.

That Hagar should feel contempt for Sarai in the transaction I think is but natural. Well might any one feel contempt for such a woman, especially after she appeals to the Lord to judge between her and her husband. At first thought you might suppose that Sarai was laying a trap for Abram in order that she might secure a divorce from him, assuming that the same laws concerning divorce prevailed at that time as they now do in the State of New York, but that was not her purpose, as the following indicates:

Genesis, Chapter 16, Verse 6.

6. But Abram said unto Sarai, Behold, thy maid is in thy hand; do to her as it pleaseth thee. And when Sarai dealt hardly with her, she fled from her face.

Of all the relationships between a man and a woman the most contemptible is that when the man refuses to protect the woman who will soon be the mother of a child of which he is the father. Sickening beyond expression is the character of a man, who, after performing the act that he did, and under the circumstances, should put the blame and the responsibility upon his wife. True, we hold neither of them in high estimation, but under all such circumstances let us at least favor the weaker of the two. We have seen the character of Abram manifested in his relation with Pharaoh and quite naturally expect him to shirk his responsibility whenever he can. That he was an adept in "hiding behind a woman's skirt" no one can deny. It has just occurred to me to inquire how many men to-day would stoop to the degradation that has so far been related about this leading Patriarch of early Biblical times. Poor Hagar is banished from the house and her only refuge is the wilderness. The Lord steps in at this point, and let us see what his intercession brings to the poor woman.

Genesis, Chapter 16, Verses 7-12.

7. And the angel of the Lord found her by a fountain of water in the wilderness, by the fountain in the way to Shur.

8. And he said, Hagar, Sarai's maid, whence camest thou? and whither wilt thou go? And she said, I flee from the face of my mistress Sarai.

9. And the angel of the Lord said unto her, Return to thy mistress, and submit thyself under her hands.

10. And the angel of the Lord said unto her, I will multiply thy seed exceedingly, that it shall not be numbered for multitude.

11. And the angel of the Lord said unto her, Behold, thou art with child, and shalt bear a son, and shalt call his name Ishmael; because the Lord hath heard thy affliction.

12. And he will be a wild man; his hand will be against every man, and every man's hand against him: and he shall dwell in the presence of all his brethren.

Enough from this chapter concerning the duplicity of Sarai and the culpability of Abram. What would we say to-day were such an example as theirs to be given to the world by our leading men and women? To-day we admire the very opposite of that which makes up the married life of this infamous couple.

Once more in the life of Abram and Sarai does Abram permit Sarai to submit to the embrace of other men for compensation and to save his miserable self. It appears that he made a business of the scheme, and from reports, shared very profitably after each transaction. One quotation of such a degrading act, I think, is sufficient for us at this time, but for the benefit of those who would like to become more fully acquainted with the life of this "Holy" pair, I advise them to read Genesis, Chapter 20. We all know what happened to Hagar for taking the "good advice" of the Lord and returning to her mistress. Both Sarai and Abram cast her out of the house and again into the wilderness with her child. Judging from this instance, the Lord's advice is not a very good thing to follow.

The blessing the Lord gave Hagar when his angel finds her in "her affliction" and "with child" was not very comforting to her either, for verse 12 says her son "will be a wild man; and his hand will be against every man, and every man's hand against him."

But on to the next story that bears a close relationship and resemblance to this one.

Chapter II.

Isaac, The Son of Abram, And His Wife Rebekah.

"Like Father, like son" -- "a chip of the old block," so to speak, seems to have been the case of Isaac, the son of Abram. Since the Lord so favored Abram for the life he led, it is no wonder that Isaac "followed his father's footsteps." For we find this gallant specimen of the early Jewish Fathers ready to do the same degrading and despicable act with his "fair to look upon" wife, Rebekah, as his father Abram did to his mother Sarai. No complaint here for lack of filial devotion. He ran "true to form" as the saying goes.

For proof I quote Genesis, Chapter 26, Verses 1-7.

1. And there was a famine in the land, besides the first famine that was in the days of Abraham. And Isaac went unto Abimelech king of the Philistines unto Gerar.

2. And the Lord appeared unto him, and said, Go not down into Egypt: dwell in the land which I shall tell thee of.

3. Sojourn in this land, and I will be with thee, and will bless thee: for unto thee, and unto thy seed, I will give all these countries, and I will perform the oath which I sware unto Abraham thy father;

4. And I will make thy seed to multiply as the stars of heaven, and will give unto thy seed all these countries; and in thy seed shall all the nations of the earth be blessed:

5. Because that Abraham obeyed my voice, and kept my charge, my commandments, my statutes, and my laws.

6. And Isaac dwelt in Gerar.

7. And the men of the place asked him of his wife; and he said, She is my sister: for he feared to say, She is my wife; lest, said he, the men of the place should kill me for Rebekah; because she was fair to look upon.

Besides Isaac inheriting his father's tendencies and following in his footsteps, he also inherited his father's ability to select pretty women. Rebekah was as "fair to look upon" as was Sarai, and it seems that both women were so fascinating that wherever they went other men coveted them. Isaac, as well as Abraham,[5] was ready and willing to prostitute his wife for protection to himself.

---

[5] Abram, is now spelled Abraham in the Bible.

Genesis, Chapter 26, Verses 8-11.

8. And it came to pass, when he had been there a long time, that Abimelech king of the Philistines looked out at a window, and saw, and, behold, Isaac was sporting with Rebekah his wife.

9. And Abimelech called Isaac, and said, Behold, of a surety she is thy wife: and how saidst thou, She is my sister? And Isaac said unto him, Because I said, Lest I die for her.

10. And Abimelech said, What is this thou hast done unto us? one of the people might lightly have lain with thy wife, and thou shouldest have brought guiltiness upon us.

11. And Abimelech charged all his people, saying, He that toucheth this man or his wile shall surely be put to death.

In Biblical times there was less occasion for the ingenuity of "peeping Toms." Houses were not built as they are to-day. Provisions for privacy were somewhat lacking. Windows and window shades were luxuries that were to be enjoyed at a much later and Pagan period.

Despite the fact that Isaac "deceived" King Abimelech as to the true relationship of Rebekah, the King nevertheless must have found it quite amusing to watch Isaac sporting with her. Abimelech significantly remarks: "Of a surety she is thy wife." What sport could a man and woman "play" so that another person can "for a surety" classify them as man and wife? The word "sporting" as used in this connection cannot fail of its intended meaning.

What a fine situation does this pretty story present to put before an inquiring and inquisitive child! Fond Parents, suppose you had taught your child to revere the Bible, and your child, being dutiful. read it for "inspiration and guidance." Suppose he chanced upon this delightful story, and being unable to grasp the subtle meaning of the word sporting as used in this connection, came to you for an explanation? What answer would you give your child? Would you deliberately lie to him and say that they were kissing each other; or would you more properly caution your child against reading a book which contained a story with such an inference. Wouldn't you consider a book that contained such a suggestive narrative utterly unfit for your child's reading?

Or is it that you yourselves are totally ignorant of what the Bible contains, and, like the rest of mankind, accept it because it has been handed down from generation to generation?

Any one who has the Bible in his home has a very questionable book in his household, and he should not be dismayed if any of his children follow the examples that are found therein.

But back to the Biblical characters for a moment, and let us engage this moment in reflection. There has been a great misunderstanding about the Bible. Instead of admiring and exalting the characters we are told to revere, we should admire and exalt the characters we are told were heathens.

Is not in this story the character of Abimelech more sterling and elevating than that of Isaac? Does he not chide Isaac for deception when he discovers that Rebekah is his wife and not his sister? Does he not censure him for the great harm he might have brought upon her? Should we admire a man who is willing to sacrifice his wife to save himself and condemn another who seeks to protect her? The ninth and tenth verses quoted in this story should be blazoned forth to all the land as an example of an unprincipled character in contrast to that of a man of sterling integrity. The severe reprimand given Isaac by Abimelech when he said: 'What is this thou has done unto us? One of the people might lightly have lain with thy wife, and thou shouldest have brought guiltiness upon us," is sufficient condemnation by Biblical testimony alone for his act.

To the fair daughters of the land, I advise them before they take a man as a husband to make sure that he does not believe too literally in the morality of the Bible, and that his attitude towards woman be of a different hue than that of the character which the religious element of the community have admonished us to follow so implicitly.

The preacher finds profit and interest in telling you about the little farce of Abraham offering this precious son, Isaac, as a sacrifice to the Lord, but they don't tell you how this same son, whom the Lord so opportunely saved, was willing to offer his wife to the lust of another without the Lord even giving it a "second thought."

I wonder where the Lord was, while this interesting scene, which Abimelech observed, was taking place. Was he also enjoying the sight of watching Isaac sporting with Rebekah?

We will now proceed to the next divinely inspired story. In this story the very lowest ebb of moral degradation is reached. To think that a book held so sacred should contain such a narrative is almost beyond comprehension.

This story, taken from the book that is supposed to be our infallible guide in all the relations of life, is really beneath contempt. But it is so necessary and essential that the world know exactly what the Bible contains that I will quote the vital parts of it to you. Comment upon this story will not be necessary, as it is one of those narratives which tell in

31

no uncertain terms their own story and worth. If this story were told with some degree of polish or merit, we might value it for its literary worth, but it is so miserable, both in its literary style and in its plot, that it is even unfit to dwell upon except to expose its degrading lesson.

Chapter III.

Incest or Lot and His Daughters.

That ministers and "messengers of the Lord" have always enjoyed privileges denied to others is a fact, despite the fact that this fact is a paradox. That "holy men," men who know least about what they pretend to know, should take precedence over the rest of mankind is an incongruity. And it is because of two such "holy men" that a father, and incidentally a grand Patriarch of the Bible, offers his daughters upon the alter of lust.

But the Bible can tell its own story best and so I quote Genesis, Chapter 19, Verses 1-7.

And there came two angels to Sodom at even; and Lot sat in the gate of Sodom: and Lot seeing them rose up to meet them; and he bowed himself with his face toward the ground;

2. And he said, Behold now, my lords, turn in, I pray you, into your servant's house, and tarry all night, and wash your feet, and ye shall rise up early, and go on your ways. And they said, Nay; but we will abide in the street all night.

3. And he pressed upon them greatly; and they turned in unto him, and entered into his house; and he made them a feast, and did bake unleavened bread, and they did eat.

4. But before they lay down, the men of the city, even the men of Sodom, compassed the house round, both old and young, all the people from every quarter:

5. And they called unto Lot, and said unto him, Where are the men which came in to thee this night? bring them out unto us, that we may know them.

6. And Lot went out at the door unto them, and shut the door after him,

7. And said, I pray you, brethren, do not so wickedly.

Being unable to satisfy the men of Sodom by persuasion, and rather than surrender these two precious "angels" to them, Lot resorted to a method which very seldom fails with "unreasonable" men. When an appeal to their manhood is of no avail many women seek death rather than suffer the embrace of their attacker, and we admire women with such courage, but that is not according to Biblical standard. This is the method the Bible advises us to pursue.

Genesis, Chapter 19, Verse 8.

8. Behold now, I have two daughters which have not known man; let me, I pray you, bring them out unto you, and do ye to them as is good in your eyes: only unto these men do nothing; for therefore came they under the shadow of my roof.

An elevating situation is this! Here is a father willing to give his two virgin daughters to an angry mob of men to "do ye to them as is good in your eyes," which simply means to rape them, provided they do not harm the two angels of the Lord.

It is important for parents who are so concerned about the moral life of their children and whose interests they have so much at heart -- especially their daughters -- to consider well this story. If parents who are believers in the Bible are concerned about the places of amusement and companions of their children, they should consider this story when they admonish them to read the Bible for guidance.

What father would follow the example of this "man of God" who, when the exigency of the circumstances just related arose, offered his daughters to be so sacrificed? I do not know what you think of a father who would give his two virgin daughters to the lust of an angry mob of men to protect two angels of the Lord, but my love of liberty deters me from telling you what I think of him.

The story continues in the Bible with God having saved Lot and his family and bringing destruction upon the people of Sodom and Gomorrah, for their wickedness. As we are not concerned with that element of the Bible at the present time it is needless to dwell upon the puerility of the narrative chronicling this event. But I do not think I will digress too far when I call your attention for a moment to the justice of God in saving and blessing a man of Lot's unprincipled character, after he had offered his two daughters upon the altar of lust.

After God had rained "fire and brimstone" upon the people of Sodom and Gomorrah and had destroyed all the inhabitants and "all that grew upon the ground," we find Lot with his wife and two daughters safe beyond the limits of destruction. We are all acquainted with what happened to Lot's wife because she desired to see what happened. I am sure we all would have done the same thing under the circumstances. It is a natural impulse, and one of the strongest of our nature. With only Lot and his two daughters left of all the inhabitants of Sodom and Gomorrah, whom you will remember God destroyed for their wickedness, let us follow closely the action of their lives and see what a beneficent example and legacy of morality they left the world. Let us also weigh in the balance God's judgment in making this selection. We now come to the most important phase of this story, and if you are ready to read the details of an incestuous union between father and daughter, read attentively what is to follow.

I am quoting from the Holy Bible, Genesis, Chapter 19, Verses 30-38.

30. And Lot went up out of Zoar, and dwelt in the mountain, and his two daughters with him; for he feared to dwell in Zoar: and he dwelt in a cave, he and his two daughters.

31. And the firstborn said unto the younger, Our father is old, and there is not a man in the earth to come in unto us after the manner of all the earth:

32. Come, let us make our father drink wine, and we will lie with him, that we may preserve seed of our father.

33. And they made their father drink wine that night: and the firstborn went in, and lay with her father; and he perceived not when she lay down, nor when she arose.

34. And it came to pass on the morrow, that the firstborn said unto the younger, Behold, I lay yesternight with my father: let us make him drink wine this night also; and go thou in, and lie with him, that we may preserve seed of our father.

35. And they made their father drink wine that night also: and the younger arose, and lay with him; and he perceived not when she lay down, nor when she arose.

36. Thus were both the daughters of Lot with child by their father.

37. And the firstborn bare a son, and called his name Moab: the same is the father of the Moabites unto this day.

38. And the younger, she also bare a son, and called his name Ben-ammi: the same is the father of the children of Ammon unto this day.

My vocabulary fails me in trying to comment properly upon this story. Just think of it! A father committing the sexual act with his own daughters and so drunk that "he perceived not when she lay down, nor when she arose!"

Is it possible that people really grasp the significance of this story? Are they aware of its gross debauchery? Can the minute details of this story be read without bringing a blush of shame to the cheeks of the reader?

Just a word to parents about this "Holy Book of God." What would you fathers and mothers say if your daughter should read the Bible and come and tell you, in detail, of this revolting episode? It is needless to ask what you would do if she brought home another book in which a story of this kind appeared. You would admonish her never to pollute her mind with such filth. If that would be your action with a book of any other title than that of "Holy Bible," to what depths of superstition have you sunk that you are so blind to its degrading influence?

Wake up, well-meaning parents, and become conscious of the obscenity to be found in this unwholesome book. A whole volume could be written about this story of Lot and his daughters, but at present we are only concerned with the act of incest.

This story of Lot and his daughters does not even contain a moral. The father to-day who is guilty of such an act is sent to prison. If he were so drunk that "he did not know when she lay down nor when she arose," it would be so much the worse for him.

This story of the Bible is too revolting to dwell upon longer except once more to impress forcibly upon you the "high elevating moral standard of its pages." I ask, is it possible for a person to read such a story, and then tell the innocent children of the race to read the Bible for moral inspiration and guidance? A story in which the very name of father is slandered, and where the pure blossom of womanhood is pictured in this degenerate manner.

Chapter IV.

Jacob, Leah and Rachel.

Integrity and faithfulness are two virtues which we cherish above all others. Deception is abhorred, no matter in what condition, or by whom it is practiced. But since Jacob is a Patriarch of the Bible and one of God's favorites, deception when practiced by him is excusable. Pardonable also is the prostitutional bickering between two wives when related in the Bible. Were such a scene to be found in any other book it would very properly be called vulgar and judged too coarse for cultural reading.

The story goes that Jacob came unto the house of Laban, who had two daughters. Leah, tender eyed, was the elder; but Rachel, the younger, was beautiful and well favoured. But let the story be told as the Bible records it.

I quote Genesis, Chapter 29, Verses 15-20.

15. And Laban said unto Jacob, Because thou art my brother, shouldest thou therefore serve me for nought? tell me, what shall thy wages be?

16. And Laban had two daughters: the name of the elder was Leah, and the name of the younger was Rachel.

17. Leah was tender eyed; but Rachel was beautiful and well favoured.

18. And Jacob loved Rachel; and said, I will serve thee seven years for Rachel thy younger daughter.

19. And Laban said, It is better that I give her to thee, than that I should give her to another man: abide with me.

20. And Jacob served seven years for Rachel; and they seemed unto him but a few days, for the love he had to her.

Now so much for the bargain. Jacob served seven years for the girl he loved. Surely such a servitude is well deserving of payment. Since there was no pretense made as to why Jacob wanted Rachel as his wife, I will quote it here.

Genesis, Chapter 29, Verse 21.

21. And Jacob said unto Laban, Give me my wife, for my days are fulfilled, that I may go in unto her.

It is needless to mention here the almost irrepressible desire to embrace his wife that obsesses a man on his wedding night, particularly when he has waited seven years to win the object of his love. But since the Bible has led us so far into the story we will let it continue with the narrative:

Genesis, Chapter 29, Verses 22-24.

22. And Laban gathered together all the men of the place, and made a feast.

23. And it came to pass in the evening, that he took Leah his daughter, and brought her to him; and he went in unto her.

24. And Laban gave unto his daughter Leah Zilpah his maid for a handmaid.

Since Leah and Rachel were not twins and since their descriptions, as Biblically described, were such as to unhesitatingly distinguish one from the other, Jacob must have been blinded by passion not to have seen that the daughter given him by Laban was not the one he had bargained for. Nevertheless, "he went in unto her," and only discovered his mistake the following morning; no doubt when the light of day shone upon her.

But back to our story, and see what happens when Jacob discovers that the woman he lay with the night before was not the one for whom he had labored seven years and was to receive as his share of the bargain. His choice was Rachel, "the beautiful and well favoured." The deception of Laban is not of interest to us at this time. Since it is Jacob's concern we will let him speak for himself.

Genesis, Chapter 29, Verse 25.

25. And it came to pass that in the morning, behold, it was Leah: and he said to Laban, What is this thou hast done unto me? did not I serve with thee for Rachel? wherefore then hast thou beguiled me?

No one can deny the fact that Jacob was perfectly justified in his complaint. For a mere pittance of another seven years of labor Laban gives Jacob, after a week's work as a bond of good faith, the daughter of his choice. But since the Bible can tell this detail of the matter better than I can, I will give way to it.

Genesis, Chapter 29, Verses 26-30.

26. And Laban said, It must not be so done in our country, to give the younger before the firstborn.

27. Fulfil her week, and we will give thee this also for the service which thou shalt serve with me yet seven other years.

28. And Jacob did so, and fulfilled her week: and he gave him Rachel his daughter to wife also.

29. And Laban gave to Rachel his daughter Bilhah his handmaid to be her maid.

30. And he went in also unto Rachel, and he loved also Rachel more than Leah, and served with him yet seven other years.

And now the Lord enters into this family affair, not to help the situation, as one would expect from an omniscient being, but to bring his curses with him.

Genesis, Chapter 29, Verse 31.

31. And when the Lord saw that Leah was hated, he opened her womb, but Rachel was barren.

The fecundity of Leah, after the Lord "opened her womb," is surely worth recording and it follows.

Genesis, Chapter 29, Verses 32-35.

32. And Leah conceived, and bare a son; and she called his name Reuben: for she said, Surely the Lord hath looked upon my affliction; now therefore my husband will love me.

33. And she conceived again, and bare a son; and said, Because the Lord hath heard that I was hated, he hath therefore given me this son also: and she called his name Simeon.

34. And she conceived again, and bare a son; and said, Now this time will my husband be joined unto me, because I have borne him three sons: therefore was his name called Levi.

35. And she conceived again, and bare a son; and she said, Now will I praise the Lord: therefore she called his name Judah; and left bearing.

Unfortunately, because of Leah's fecundity, Rachel becomes jealous of her sister and demands of Jacob that she, too, bear him a child. Jacob chides her for demanding of him that which he would be only too willing to give, but the fault lies with her. As fecund as was her sister so sterile was she. But a peculiar method is pursued by the Biblical female characters when they find themselves unable to bear children. This method prevailed in the household of Abram and Sarai and I see no reason why it should not be permissible in the polygamous household of Jacob, Leah and Rachel.

Genesis, Chapter 30, Verses 1-4.

And when Rachel saw that she bare Jacob no children, Rachel envied her sister; and said unto Jacob, Give me children, or else I die.

2. And Jacob's anger was kindled against Rachel; and he said, Am I in God's stead, who hath withheld from thee the fruit of the womb?

3. And she said, Behold my maid Bilhah, go in unto her; and she shall bear upon my knees, that I may also have children by her.

4. And she gave him Bilhah her handmaid to wife: and Jacob went in unto her.

Like Abraham, Jacob lost no time in complying with the wishes of Rachel to "go in unto" Bilhah, her handmaid. What an accommodating arrangement must have prevailed for the Biblical men of old. No wonder we have agitations to go "Back to Methuselah."

But to record the progeny of Jacob we continue to quote

Genesis, Chapter 30, Verses 5-8.

5. And Bilhah conceived, and bare Jacob a son.

6. And Rachel said, God hath judged me, and hath also heard my voice, and hath given me a son: therefore called she his name Dan.

7. And Bilhah Rachel's maid conceived again, and bare Jacob a second son.

8. And Rachel said, With great wrestlings have I wrestled with my sister, and I have prevailed: and she called his name Naphtali.

That must have been a spectacular wrestling match between Leah and Rachel. But Leah was not to be outdone, and when she could no longer bear children, gives Jacob Zilpah, her handmaid, to continue the race in her desperation to overcome the comeliness of her sister.

Genesis, Chapter 30, Verses 9-13.

9. When Leah saw that she had left bearing, she took Zilpah her maid, and gave her Jacob to wife.

10. And Zilpah Leah's maid bare Jacob a son.

11. And Leah said, A troop cometh: and she called his name Gad.

12. And Zilpah Leah's maid bare Jacob a second son.

13. And Leah said, Happy am I, for the daughters will call me blessed: and she called his name Asher.

In the 11th verse just mentioned I believe there must be a mistake regarding the number of children Zilpah, Leah's maid, bore at this time. To quote: "And Leah said, A troop cometh; and she called his name Gad." Judging from the word "troop" I was led to believe that she was to bear twins or triplets, but again, I suppose I must confess my lack of spiritual understanding.

A situation which I believe quite unparalleled in the literature of the land and sufficient unto itself without further comment, follows.

Genesis, Chapter 30, Verses 14-16.

14. And Reuben went in the days of wheat harvest, and found mandrakes in the field, and brought them unto his mother Leah. Then Rachel said to Leah, Give me, I pray thee, of thy son's mandrakes.

15. And she said unto her, Is it a small matter that thou hast taken my husband? and wouldest thou take away my son's mandrakes also? And Rachel said, Therefore he shall lie with thee to night for thy son's mandrakes.

16. And Jacob came out of the field in the evening, and Leah went out to meet him, and said, Thou must come in unto me; for surely I have hired thee with my son's mandrakes. And he lay with her that night.

For a sister to bribe a sister with the sweat of her son's labor for the privilege of sexual intercourse with her own husband is too coarse an act of prostitution for me to comment upon further. Can you find in any book other than the Bible such a despicable bargaining?

"And Rachel said, Therefore he shall lie with thee to-night for thy son's mandrakes.

"And Jacob came out of the field in the evening, and Leah went out to meet him, and said, Thou must come in unto me; for surely I have hired thee with my son's mandrakes." And the Bible does not hesitate to say that "he lay with her that night!"

To dwell upon the degrading custom of polygamy as was practiced in the early Biblical days is not exactly within the scope of this work, and for that reason I will leave unmentioned some of the recorded instances of this condemned institution.

I cannot understand how public men, men of learning and experience, can insist that the Bible, which contains the stories quoted that shock even the vulgar-minded, should be our pre-eminent guide in all earthly affairs, and that it should not only be read by, but actually taught to the growing generation in search of high moral ethics.

Chapter V.

The Rape of Dinah.

Since the Biblical narrations thus far have contained stories of lust, incest, infidelity, and prostitution surely a story of rape is not out of place and I therefore proceed to relate the story of the rape of Dinah, the daughter of Leah, who was the un-bargained-for and unwanted wife of Jacob, by young Shechem, the son of Hamor the Hivite.

Rape is a delicate subject and should be delicately handled. Even in our Courts of law it is considered of such a nature that the general public is not permitted in the court room during its recital. What then must be said when such a story is found prominently related in the Bible, a book which is reverentially impressed upon our children as being "a divine revelation from God"? Could a more obnoxious and offensive story than that of rape be put into the hands of the young?

This story alone is sufficient to condemn the Bible as being unfit to inculcate moral instruction in children. Since the story is found in the Bible and is not the result of my imagination, I will proceed with it.

I quote the Scriptures, Genesis, Chapter 34, Verses 1-2.

And Dinah the daughter of Leah, which she bare unto Jacob, went out to see the daughters of the land.

2. And when Shechem the son of Hamor the Hivite, prince of the country, saw her, he took her, and lay with her, and defiled her.

So much for the act of rape, and what followed I consider of equal importance and will proceed.

Genesis, Chapter 34, Verse 3.

3. And his soul crave unto Dinah the daughter of Jacob, and he loved the damsel and spake kindly unto the damsel.

Surely here is a situation that deserves at least our respect. If a man, unable to control his passion towards the irresistible witchery of a girl, realizes his mistake and is willing to protect her not only with his name but also with his love, what should be our attitude towards him? Especially so, when the girl, the object of his passion and his love, willingly accedes to his proposal.

A fair and just and equitable offer should be met with the acceptance it deserves.

Genesis, Chapter 34, Verses 4-12.

4. And Shechem spake unto his father Hamor, saying, Get me this damsel to wife.

5. And Jacob heard that he had defiled Dinah his daughter: now his sons were with his cattle in the field: and Jacob held his peace until they were come.

6. And Hamor the father of Shechem went out unto Jacob to commune with him.

7. And the sons of Jacob came out of the field when they heard it: and the men were grieved, and they were very wroth, because he had wrought folly in Israel in lying with Jacob's daughter; which thing ought not to be done.

8. And Hamor communed with them, saying, The soul of my son Shechem longeth for your daughter: I pray you give her to him to wife.

9. And make ye marriages with us, and give your daughters unto us, and take our daughters unto you.

10. And ye shall dwell with us: and the land shall be before you; dwell and trade ye therein, and get you possessions therein.

11. And Shechem said unto her father and unto her brethren, Let me find grace in your eyes, and what ye shall say unto me I will give.

12. Ask me never so much dowry and gift, and I will give according as ye shall say unto me: but give me the damsel to wife.

Surely no man could plead his suit more earnestly nor with more sincerity than young Shechem; nor do more to atone for the act of his impetuous youth.

What can a man more honorably offer than "Ask me never so much dowry and gift, and I will give according as ye shall say unto me"? He pleaded his cause with fervor, ardor, and honesty, and if Justice is blind as some say, and the scales faulty, he did not deserve the brutal retaliation which the sons of Jacob inflicted upon him, his family and his country.

But we are getting a bit ahead of our story and must continue to quote the Scriptures. Now here is what Jacob and his sons demanded of Shechem and Hamor as reparation for his deed.

Genesis, Chapter 34, Verses 13-18.

13. And the sons of Jacob answered Shechem and Hamor his father deceitfully, and said, because he had defiled Dinah their sister:

14. And they said unto them, We cannot to this thing, to give our sister to one that is uncircumcised; for that were a reproach unto us:

15. But in this will we consent unto you: If ye will be as we be, that every male of you be circumcised;

16. Then will we give our daughters unto you, and we will take your daughters to us, and we will dwell with you, and we will become one people.

17. But if ye will not hearken unto us, to be circumcised; then will we take our daughter, and we will be gone.

18. And their words pleased Hamor and Shechem Hamor's son.

Circumcision is the price demanded! Honor, Love and Protection are subordinate to the existence of a foreskin! The ritual of a creed is of more transcendent importance than anything else within the power of man to give! Think of it! More important than peace, friendliness and the happiness of not only a race but of the entire country. Anxious to keep his pledge of "never so much dowry and gift" to win the object of his love and make amends for his misdeed young Shechem complied immediately with their demand as the following testifies.

Genesis, Chapter 34, Verse 19.

19. And the young man deferred not to do the thing, because he had delight in Jacob's daughter: and he was more honourable than all the house of his father.

That he was more honorable than all the house of his father is not true according to the following testimony: Genesis, Chapter 34, Verses 20-24.

20. And Hamor and Shechem his son came unto the gate of their city, and communed with the men of their city, saying,

21. These men are peaceable with us; therefore let them dwell in the land, and trade therein; for the land, behold, it is large enough for them; let us take their daughters to us for wives, and let us give them our daughters.

22. Only herein will the men consent unto us for to dwell with us, to be one people, if every male among us be circumcised, as they are circumcised.

23. Shall not their cattle and their substance and every beast of theirs be ours? only let us consent unto them, and they will dwell with us.

24. And unto Hamor and unto Shechem his son hearkened all that went out of the gate of his city; and every male was circumcised, all that went out of the gate of his city.

Is there recorded in all history a more honorable compliance with the demands of another than that just quoted of the House of Hamor? But this was not enough and did not satisfy the savage cravings of Jacob's sons, and if you read carefully of what went before you would have pondered over verse 13, of this chapter.

Let me repeat it for your benefit: "And the sons of Jacob answered Shechem and his father deceitfully."

And now follows the most diabolical crime ever perpetrated upon an innocent people, particularly when done in the name of Peace. I call the attention of those ardent peace lovers who use the Bible in their deliberations to this passage. As you probably are not acquainted with the deviltry of the Biblical characters or with what cunning savageness they can inflict punishment, I will quote it verbatim to you.

Genesis, Chapter 34, Verses 25-29.

25. And it came to pass on the third day, when they were sore, that two of the sons of Jacob, Simeon and Levi, Dinah's brethren, took each man his sword, and came upon the city boldly, and slew all the males.

26. And they slew Hamor and Shechem his son with the edge of the sword, and took Dinah out of Shechem's house, and went out.

27. The sons of Jacob came upon the slain, and spoiled the city, because they had defiled their sister.

28. They took their sheep, and their oxen, and their asses, and that which was in the city, and that which was in the field,

29. And all their wealth, and all their little ones, and their wives took they captive, and spoiled even all that was in the house.

And this is a sample of Biblical ethics, Biblical morals, Biblical justice!

Well might Jacob say that this deed makes him stink among the inhabitants of the land. Since this is a Biblical expression, let me quote it.

Genesis, Chapter 34, Verses 30-31.

30. And Jacob said to Simeon and Levi, Ye have troubled me to make me to stink among the inhabitants of the land, among the Canaanites and the Perizzites: and I being few in number, they shall gather themselves together against me, and slay me; and I shall be destroyed, I and my house.

A pitiable justification cannot condone this foul deed. Its stench pollutes the entire volume and not only nauseates the reader but contaminates the very pages upon which it is written. All ye Ministers, Priests and Rabbis, what say ye of this vicious story and the vicious book in which it is printed? Are ye stunned into speechlessness by its atrociousness?

Chapter VI.

Joseph and Potiphar's Wife.

The story of Joseph is familiar to us; that is, he being Jacob's favorite son, his father made him a coat of many colors; and how his brothers being jealous, put him into a pit to starve to death. But for fear that their crime would be detected, they decided instead to sell him to the Egyptians. After the consummation of this business transaction and with full satisfaction of their revenge, his brothers sought a plausible explanation to Jacob for the disappearance of his favorite child. Their explanation was "clever," to say the least. They took Joseph's famous coat of many colors, which his father had given him, and killing a tender goat, smeared it with the blood of the animal. This blood-smeared coat they took to their father and told him that Joseph was killed, and of course Jacob believed it. And this, despite the fact that Jacob was on intimate terms with God. It appears that God did not want to tell him the truth of the matter. He evidently wanted as the English would say, to spoof him. That Joseph's brothers sold him at a bargain price can be imagined, as he was quickly resold into bondage and we find him in the possession of a man by the name of Potiphar. What transpires during Joseph's servitude in the household of Potiphar particularly concerns us in the story of this famous Biblical character.

I will not make much comment upon the story, nor the plot, nor the characters mentioned, but will record it for the purpose of showing that it contains a bit of "snappy" fiction, and advise those who purchase magazines containing such stories, and who relish the lascivious, to skip next month's issue and purchase instead a copy of the Bible.

I quote Genesis, Chapter 39, Verses 1-6.

And Joseph was brought down to Egypt; and Potiphar, an officer of Pharaoh, captain of the guard, an Egyptian, bought him of the hands of the Ishmaelites, which had brought him down thither.

2. And the Lord was with Joseph, and he was a prosperous man; and he was in the house of his master the Egyptian.

3. And his master saw that the Lord was with him, and that the Lord made all that he did to prosper in his hand.

4. And Joseph found grace in his sight, and he served him: and he made him overseer over his house, and all that he had he put into his hand.

5. And it came to pass from the time that he had made him overseer in his house, and over all that he had, that the Lord blessed the

Egyptian's house for Joseph's sake; and the blessing of the Lord was upon all that he had in the house, and in the field.

6. And he left all that he had in Joseph's hand; and he knew not aught he had, save the bread which he did eat. And Joseph was a goodly person, and well favoured.

If the Lord "blessed the Egyptian's (Potiphar's) house for Joseph's sake, and the blessing of the Lord was upon all that he had in the house, and in the field," where were the Lord's "blessings" when the following tête-à-tête took place?

Genesis, Chapter 39, Verse 7.

7. And it came to pass after these things, that his master's wife cast her eyes upon Joseph; and she said, Lie with me.

What a compromising situation that must have been! But on with this thrilling adventure.

Genesis, Chapter 39, Verses 8-9.

8. But he refused, and said unto his master's wife, Behold, my master wotteth not what is with me in the house, and he hath committed all that he hath to my hand;

9. There is none greater in this house than I; neither hath he kept back any thing from me but thee, because thou art his wife; how then can I do this great wickedness, and sin against God?

Admirable, young man, admirable. Would that all men were like you. Just think, if every man were a "Joseph," there would be absolutely no divorces granted, at least in the State of New York. But the fair lady was too fascinated with our young hero and persisted in her seduction, as we gather from the following.

Genesis, Chapter 39, Verse 10.

10. And it came to pass, as she spake to Joseph day by day, that he hearkened not unto her, to lie by her, or to be with her.

What a great moral hazard did this young man experience day after day. It seems an almost irresistible temptation to hear the subdued tones and feel the warm breath of a passionate woman tremulously crying, "Lie with me! Lie with me! Lie with me!" But ah! The plot thickens and the dramatic climax is almost at hand.

Genesis, Chapter 39, Verses 11-12.

11. *And it came to pass about this time, that Joseph went into the house to do his business; and there was none of the men of the house there within.*

12. *And she caught him by his garment, saying, Lie with me: and he left his garment in her hand, and fled, and got him out.*

Mrs. Potiphar, unable to satisfy her passionate longing with the object of her desire, now seeks to protect herself, in this embarrassing situation, with an explanation to her husband of the affair in the following manner.

Genesis, Chapter 39, Verses 13-16.

13. *And it came to pass, when she saw that he had left his garment in her hand, and was fled forth,*

14. *That she called unto the men of her house, and spake unto them, saying, See, he hath brought in a Hebrew unto us to mock us; he came in unto me to lie with me, and I cried with a loud voice:*

15. *And it came to pass, when he heard that I lifted up my voice and cried, that he left his garment with me, and fled, and got him out.*

16. *And she laid up his garment by her, until his lord came home.*

This story has the eternal triangle for its plot, and those who seek narrations where the marriage tie is violated cannot get a more delicious morsel of scandal than this one. There are many points in this story of Joseph and Potiphar's wife that we could dwell upon at length; especially of Joseph running out of the house, after leaving his garment in the hands of Mrs. Potiphar, and what a fine sight he must have been after such a perilous encounter!

And again, there is the awkward position of Mrs. Potiphar standing in all her loveliness, holding Joseph's garment without Joseph! The balance of the story merely relates that Potiphar believed Mrs. Potiphar's version of the story and sent our hero to jail. All this happened, mind you, under the benediction of God as stated in the fifth verse of this chapter. Let me refresh your memory with it. "The Lord blessed the Egyptian's house for Joseph's sake; and the blessing of the Lord was upon all that he had in the house and in the field." If the blessing of the Lord produced the results we have just recounted, his blessing would seem to be of questionable value.

But whatever the taste of those seeking this kind of amusement in the reading they select, I wonder if you would give such a story to your son and daughter to draw their moral inspiration from? You fond Parents, who so sacredly fondle the Bible, do you ever stop to think of the probability of your son or daughter reading this story in his or her study of it? Particularly would the story of Joseph be read because the name of Joseph has become celebrated in Biblical history.

Chapter VII.

Judah and His Daughter-in-law Tamar.

In my introduction to this book, I warned those who felt that if their sensibilities might be shocked by anything that would be said in the discussion of my subject, not to read this book; and if in the citation of the story to follow you are brought face to face with an obnoxious situation you cannot blame me for the sickening disgust you will feel at the conclusion of this narrative.

It is not my purpose to bring your attention to these immoral stories of the Bible because they are vulgar, but for the purpose of bringing your attention to what an abomination it is to insist that our children read the Bible in order to get a proper understanding of life. My deep concern is to relate the licentious acts of the celebrated characters of this infamous book and bring them parallel to, and into comparison with, our present standard for the same relationship.

I quote Genesis, Chapter 38, Verses 1-5.

And it came to pass at that time, that Judah went down from his brethren, and turned in to a certain Adullamite, whose name *was* Hirah.

2. And Judah saw there a daughter of a certain Canaanite, whose name was Shuah; and he took her, and went in unto her.

3. And she conceived, and bare a son; and he called his name Er.

4. And she conceived again, and bare a son; and she called his name Onan.

5. And she yet again conceived, and bare a son; and called his name Shelah: and he was at Chezib, when she bare him.

I do not think it out of place to make mention of the fact that the method and mode of expression used in the Bible to denote the marital relationship and the subsequent birth of a child, is in itself an indelicacy that deserves our condemnation. Would it not have been better to say: "And Judah saw there a daughter of a certain Canaanite, whose name was Shuah, and he married her and their first child was called Er, and the second Onan and the third Shelah"?

Wouldn't such a description be more conducive to refinement and moral betterment than the expression that "he went in unto her, and she conceived"? Instead of the Bible's avoiding those expressions that are inelegant, particular pains were taken to use them and use them pronouncedly.

Genesis, Chapter 38, Verses 6-7.

6. And Judah took a wife for Er his firstborn, whose name was Tamar.

7. And Er, Judah's firstborn, was wicked in the sight of the Lord; and the Lord slew him.

As I am one of the poor unfortunates who cannot understand God's ways, I am unable to perceive why he killed Er. It may be because the young man loved his wife and honored her and sought to protect her, and as this might possibly interfere with "God's plan" it was necessary to kill him. Who knows?

But let us continue, and possibly in the following verses we may obtain a glimpse of the reason why God judged Er wicked and killed him. Was it for the reason that he did not want to raise a large family?

Genesis, Chapter 38, Verses 8,10.

8. And Judah said unto Onan, Go in unto thy brother's wife, and marry her, and raise up seed to thy brother.

10. And the thing which he did displeased the Lord wherefore he slew him also.

I must refrain from quoting verse 9 of this chapter because, in my opinion, it violates statute 211 of the United States Criminal Code, which says in part:

"Every obscene, lewd or lascivious and every filthy book, pamphlet, picture, paper, letter, writing, print, or publication of any indecent character, ... designated, adapted or intended for preventing conception ... or described in a manner calculated to lead another to use or apply it for preventing conception ... and every written or printed card, letter, circular, book, pamphlet, advertisement or notice of any kind giving information, directly or indirectly, ... or how or by what means conception may be prevented; and every description calculated to induce or incite a person to so use or apply, is hereby declared to be non-mailable matter, and shall not be conveyed in the mails or delivered from any Post Office or by any letter carrier."

However strange it may seem there is in the Holy Bible a verse, which appears to me, to come within the very scope and body of the prohibition of the law just quoted; but no one seems to have requested the exclusion of the Holy Bible from the privilege of the United States mails, or is it possible that no one knew of this passage in the pages of the Holy Scriptures?

If the Bible containing this information is permitted the use of the mails what objection can be found to the dissemination of scientific information of the prevention of conception as advocated by Margaret Sanger and other Birth Control advocates?

But as this is but a side incident to this narrative, let us continue the main story.

Genesis, Chapter 38, Verse 11.

11. Then said Judah to Tamar his daughter in law, Remain a widow at thy father's house, till Shelah my son be grown: for he said, Lest peradventure he die also as his brethren did. And Tamar went and dwelt in her father's house.

For what is to follow I invite your serious attention.

Genesis, Chapter 38, Verses 12-14.

12. And in process of time the daughter of Shuah Judah's wife died; and Judah was comforted, and went up unto his sheepshearers to Timnath, he and his friend Hirah the Adullamite.

13. And it was told Tamar, saying, Behold, thy father in law goeth up to Timnath to shear his sheep.

14. And she put her widow's garments off from her, and covered her with a vail, and wrapped herself, and sat in an open place, which is by the way to Timnath; for she saw that Shelah was grown, and she was not given unto him to wife.

According to the promise of Judah, Tamar was to have as a husband, Shelah, his youngest son, when he grew to manhood. The reason why this promise was not fulfilled may be due to the fact that in the meantime Judah's wife had died and Tamar must be left free for the act that is to follow, although I do not think being married to his son would have been a barrier to the unscrupulous Judah, in his passionate quest for concupiscence.

Genesis, Chapter 38, Verses 15-16.

15. When Judah saw her, he thought her to be a harlot; because she had covered her face.

16. And he turned unto her by the way, and said, Go to, I pray thee, let me come in unto thee; (for he knew not that she was his daughter in law:) and she said, What wilt thou give me, that thou mayest come in unto me?

Certainly a prostitutional bargaining between father-in-law and daughter-in-law is not out of place in the Bible and we will proceed further with it to the culmination which naturally and inevitably follows. But let us for the continuity of the scene repeat the above dialogue. "Go to, I pray thee, let me come in unto thee." And she said, "What wilt thou give me, that thou mayest come in unto me?"

Genesis, Chapter 38, Verses 17-18.

17. And he said, I will send thee a kid from the flock. And she said, Wilt thou give me a pledge, till thou send it?

18. And he said, What pledge shall I give thee? And she said, Thy signet, and thy bracelets, and thy staff that is in thine hand. And he gave it her, and came in unto her, and she conceived by him.

Surely this is a unique story and possesses many distinct features which are not generally incorporated in "snappy stories." But as there is more to it, I will continue to quote.

Genesis, Chapter 38, Verses 19-23.

19. And she arose, and went away, and laid by her vail from her, and put on the garments of her widowhood.

20. And Judah sent the kid by the hand of his friend the Adullamite, to receive his pledge from the woman's hand: but he found her not.

21. Then he asked the men of that place, saying, Where is the harlot, that was openly by the way side? And they said, There was no harlot in this place.

22. And he returned to Judah, and said, I cannot find her; and also the men of the place said, that there was no harlot in this place.

23. And Judah said, Let her take it to her, lest we be shamed: behold, I sent this kid, and thou hast not found her.

Judah is fearful that he be "shamed" unless the harlot be found and she return to him his pledge that she demanded of him for the fulfillment of the promise to send her a token for the privilege accorded him "to come in unto her." What an embarrassment this must have been to this leading citizen of that time. Actually "caught with the goods" in his illicit sexual relationship. Just think what would have been heaped upon him had the "newspapers" gotten hold of this bit of scandal and exposed him and held him up to scorn and ridicule before all the people?

Genesis, Chapter 38, Verse 24.

24. And it came to pass about three months after, that it was told Judah, saying, Tamar thy daughter in law hath played the harlot; and also, behold, she is with child by whoredom. And Judah said, Bring her forth, and let her be burnt.

If Tamar is with child by whoredom, then Judah, this patriarch of the Jews, and one of the leading Biblical characters, and ancestor of Jesus Christ, is the father of the child in embryo. But let us go a little further in the analysis of this Man of God. In the preceding verses we noted that Judah was exceedingly anxious about his reputation and felt gravely concerned when he failed to receive back his pledge which he had given for the consummation of his sexual entertainment. But when he is informed that Tamar, his daughter-in-law, "is with child by whoredom" he shouts: "Bring her forth and let her be burnt!" Since Judah requests Tamar be brought forth we will comply with his wishes.

Genesis, Chapter 38, Verse 25.

25. When she was brought forth, she sent to her father in law, saying, By the man, whose these are, am I with child: and she said, Discern, I pray thee, whose are these, the signet and bracelets, and staff.

His "righteous indignation" quickly vanishes when she presents him with proof of his fornication. "Bring her forth and let her be burnt" does not apply when the evidence presented is "By the man whose these are am I with child"!

Genesis, Chapter 38, Verse 26.

26. And Judah acknowledged them, and said, She hath been more righteous than I; because that I gave her not to Shelah my son. And he knew her again no more.

That Tamar was not burnt because she was "with child by whoredom" was for the simple reason that Judah was both her accomplice and judge. If Judah had not been caught in this crime by actual evidence, he would have made Tamar pay the penalty of death by burning, when he was the culprit responsible for her condition and equally guilty as a participator.

As a final act of restitution Judah "knew her (Tamar) no more." The birth of one child by whoredom is always an event, but, and I might use a Biblical expression, and say, when a "troop cometh" it is a still greater occasion; for the impregnation as implanted by Judah when "he went in unto" Tamar, resulted in the birth of twins. The following quotation records the final chapter of this elevating and inspirational story.

Genesis, Chapter 38, Verses 27-29.

27. And it came to pass in the time of her travail, that, behold, twins were in her womb.

28. And it came to pass, when she travailed, that the one put out his hand: and the midwife took and bound upon his hand a scarlet thread, saying, This came out first.

29. And it came to pass, as he drew back his hand, that, behold, his brother came out: and she said, How hast thou broken forth? this breach be upon thee: therefore his name was called Pharez.

What the poor innocent child did for the midwife to cry: "The breach upon thee: therefore his name was called Pharez" is another of those Biblical incongruities that my lack of spiritual understanding prevents me from comprehending.

Genesis, Chapter 38, Verse 30.

30. And afterwards came out his brother, that had the scarlet thread upon his hand: and his name was called Zerach.

Just a few words of comment upon the story we have just concluded. Judah is one of the leading characters of the Bible. His name is honored and respected. He is one of the "Chosen People."

A leader of the race admitting licentious and criminal relations with his daughter-in-law, and hypocritically withholding punishment because he himself was particeps criminis. Let us reflect for a moment and see what acts of this man's character make his name so venerated in Jewish history? Do you remember in verse 24 when he was informed that "Tamar, his daughter-in-law is with child by whoredom," he cried, "Bring her forth and let her be burnt"? When she is brought forth to receive the wrath and sentence of the elders for prostitution, and in defense she presents the signet, the bracelets and the staff of Judah and murmurs, "By the man whose these are am I with child," this impostor and reprobate, realizing that he is as guilty as she, absolves her of all guilt in the transaction and reforms himself to the extent that "he knew her again no more."

A fine sample of manhood!

Any man, sitting upon the bench in our Courts of Law, who urges the Bible be read to our children as a source of moral inspiration should be forced to read the Bible for his own enlightenment. The drunken bawd could not let fall from his lips a more "entertaining" story to the "jury of his peers" than this insulting episode as related in the Bible.

I cannot really think it possible that there are parents actually acquainted with the Bible and the stories it contains, who permit it in their homes within reach of their children.

58

I particularly call the attention of the Reverend John Roach Straton, the man who said recently that New York was Hell with the lid raised, to this story of Tamar and Judah. Isn't he acquainted with the fact that the Bible is being freely circulated and that there are thousands of churches whose ministers are actually forcing this book upon the people, himself included? If the ministers of the gospel are too dense and stupid to realize the moral mischief resulting from the perverse teachings of the Bible, then it is about time to bring them to their senses.

Chapter VIII.

The 19th Chapter of Judges.

Why a story of this kind should be in the Bible is not difficult to understand. It would be out of place anywhere else. Although it has absolutely no connection with any act that has the slightest semblance to anything that has any bearing in any way with moral teaching, it is nevertheless quite a proper episode for the Bible to relate. It has not only no moral purport, but is absolutely devoid of anything that would make it celebrated as an immoral story. It is so repugnant to our present-day understanding that its notice in this book is merely for the purpose of calling your attention to it, and making you cognizant of the stories with which the Bible is filled.

The only thing about this story that gives it any relationship to the other stories of the Bible, is the fact that it is similar in plot, construction and view-point to that of "Lot and His Daughters." I believe it was written by the same man, who was obsessed with the libidinous, and whose hobby it was to tell such stories. Again the same monstrous sacrifice of offering a virgin daughter to satisfy the anger of a mob of men, who objected to the sheltering of a stranger. The only difference between this story and that of "Lot and His Daughters" is that the man in the lot story was "an angel of the Lord," while in this narrative the sheltered party is merely a stranger. I think it well for Biblical scholars to note the connection between them. To me, as I say, it appears that they were both written by the same man. And if they were, can it be possible that one story appears in the first part of the book of Genesis, and one after the celebrated strong man of the Bible, the herculean Samson, a lapse, according to Biblical history, of more than a thousand years? The difference of time between the two stories, as they appear in the Bible, makes it utterly impossible that the same man could have lived during both periods.

But I suppose if it appears in the Bible it is a miracle and that is a satisfactory explanation for the faithful. Since the language used in this story is so elevating and so in keeping with the Biblical standard, and so essential for the inculcation of high ethical principles in the minds of our school children, I will not mar the narrative with my own language, but will quote it as it appears.

The Book of Judges, Chapter 19, Verses 1-2.

And it came to pass in those days, when there was no king in Israel, that there was a certain Levite sojourning on the side of mount Ephraim, who took to him a concubine out or Beth-lehem-judah.

2. And his concubine played the whore against him, and went away from him unto her father's house to Beth-lehem-judah, and there were four whole months.

For the benefit of those readers who would like a full and complete explanation of the word "whore," I refer them to the Standard Dictionary, which, among other things says that it is a word "now excluded from polite speech."

Mind you, a word "now excluded from polite speech," is one of the favorite expressions of the Bible. Do you think the word represents a delicate or an inspiring thought? If you do not, why do you reverence the Bible, since it so often repeats the expression?

Do you need any reasons why the dictionary says that the word is "now excluded from polite speech"? And should a book that so often repeats a word now excluded from polite speech be held sacred above everything else in life?

But to continue. The Book of Judges, Chapter 19, Verses 3-9.

3. And her husband arose, and went after her, to speak friendly unto her, and to bring her again, having his servant with him, and a couple of asses: and she brought him into her father's house; and when the father of the damsel saw him, he rejoiced to meet him.

4. And his father in law, the damsel's father, retained him; and he abode with him three days: so they did eat and drink, and lodged there.

5. And it came to pass on the fourth day, when they arose early in the morning, that he rose up to depart: and the damsel's father said unto his son in law, Comfort thine heart with a morsel of bread, and afterward go your way.

6. And they sat down, and did eat and drink both of them together: for the damsel's father had said unto the man, Be content, I pray thee, and tarry all night, and let thine heart be merry.

7. And when the man rose up to depart, his father in law urged him: therefore he lodged there again.

8. And he arose early in the morning on the fifth day to depart: and the damsel's father said, Comfort thine heart, I pray thee. And they tarried until afternoon, and they did eat both of them.

9. And when the man rose up to depart, he, and his concubine, and his servant, his father in law, the damsel's father, said unto him, Behold, now the day draweth toward evening, I pray you tarry all night: behold, the day groweth to an end, lodge here, that thine heart may be merry; and to-morrow get you early on your way, that thou mayest go home.

This so-called diary of the woman's father and her keeper for the few days of his sojourn is truly monotonous compared to what transpired during the four months of whoredom, of which we have no record. But as I do not wish to skip any part of this story before its conclusion, you must be patient with the recital of common, inconsequential events until we come to those parts which are so horrible and shocking to our moral sense.

The Book of Judges, Chapter 19, Verses 10-12.

10. But the man would not tarry that night, but he rose up and departed, and came over against Jebus, which is Jerusalem; and there were with him two asses saddled, his concubine also was with him.

11. And when they were by Jebus, the day was far spent; and the servant said unto his master, Come, I pray thee, and let us turn in into this city of the Jebusites, and lodge in it.

12. And his master said unto him, We will not turn aside hither into the city of a stranger, that is not of the children of Israel; we will pass over to Gibeah.

There may have been a good and sufficient reason why this Israelite and his concubine did not enter "the city of the stranger."

The Book of Judges, Chapter 19, Verses 13-18.

13. And he said unto his servant, Come and let us draw near to one of these places to lodge all night, in Gibeah, or in Ramah.

14. And they passed on and went their way; and the sun went down upon them when they were by Gibeah, which belongeth to Benjamin.

15. And they turned aside thither, to go in and to lodge in Gibeah: and when he went in, he sat him down in a street of the city: for there was no man that took them into his house to lodging.

16. And, behold, there came an old man from his work out of the field at even, which was also of mount Ephraim; and he sojourned in Gibeah: but the men of the place were Benjamites.

17. And when he had lifted up his eyes, he saw a wayfaring man in the street of the city: and the old man said, Whither goest thou? and whence comest thou?

18. And he said unto him, We are passing from Beth-lehem-judah toward the side of mount Ephraim; from thence am I: and I went to

Beth-lehem-judah, but I am now going to the house of the Lord; and there is no man that receiveth me to house.

Were an ordinary stranger to knock at your door and ask for shelter, there would be some doubt about giving him succor, but let him tell you he is of the same religious belief as you are and you immediately exert your best efforts to comfort him. And this, despite the fact that very often the thief quotes Scripture, and merely uses this knowledge to gain access to your home. Our friend, the Israelite, utilized this principle of psychology with much success, as recorded in the following.

The Book of Judges, Chapter 19, Verses 19-23.

19. Yet there is both straw and provender for our asses; and there is bread and wine also for me, and for thy handmaid, and for the young man which is with thy servants: there is no want of any thing.

20. And the old man said, Peace be with thee; howsoever, let all thy wants lie upon me; only lodge not in the street.

21. So he brought him into his house, and gave provender unto the asses: and they washed their feet, and did eat and drink.

22. Now as they were making their hearts merry, behold, the men of the city, certain sons of Belial, beset the house round about, and beat at the door, and spake to the master of the house, the old man, saying, Bring forth the man that came into thine house, that we may know him.

23. And the man, the master of the house, went out unto them, and said unto them, Nay, my brethren, nay, I pray you, do not so wickedly; seeing that this man is come into mine house, do not this folly.

Certainly it is right to protect the lonely and the weary, but this story is not written to soften our hearts for the unfortunates of the world. It has an altogether different purpose, as you will see, from the price this Biblical benefactor was willing to pay to give shelter to a stranger.

The Book of Judges, Chapter 19, Verse 24.

24. Behold, here is my daughter a maiden, and his concubine; them I will bring out now, and humble ye them, and do with them what seemeth good unto you: but unto this man do not so vile a thing.

Surely the anger of men, or if you prefer, their perversion, must indeed be deep seated, when they refuse to accept such a coveted prize as a virgin "to do what seemeth good unto you," merely for the purpose of keeping their peace.

The Book of Judges, Chapter 19, Verse 25.

25. But the men would not hearken to him: so the man took his concubine, and brought her forth unto them; and they knew her, and abused her all the night until the morning: and when the day began to spring, they let her go.

The men refused to take the virgin, for what reason I do not know, but the poor concubine "they abused all night until the morning," which by the way, is certainly a delicate and spiritual experience to be related to our growing youths. But to our story:

The Book of Judges, Chapter 19, Verses 26-27.

26. Then came the woman in the dawning of the day, and fell down at the door of the man's house where her lord was, till it was light.

27. And her lord rose up in the morning, and opened the doors of the house, and went out to go his way: and behold, the woman his concubine was fallen down at the door of the house, and her hands were upon the threshold.

What the poor woman must have suffered at the hands of these beastly men cannot be pictured in words. The poignancy of suffering; her pains, agony and despair, are beyond description.

The Book of Judges, Chapter 19, Verses 28-30.

28. And he said unto her, Up, and let us be going. But none answered. Then the man took her up upon an ass, and the man rose up, and get him unto his place.

29. And when he was come into his house, he took a knife, and laid hold on his concubine, and divided her, together with her bones, into twelve pieces, and sent her into all the coasts of Israel.

30. And it was so, that all that saw it said, There was no such deed done nor seen from the day that the children of Israel came up out of the land of Egypt unto this day: consider of it, take advice, and speak your minds.

What a fearful tragedy is this! What moral benefit can there be in telling such a story? What moral good can our children receive from the reading of this inhuman, brutal and degrading episode? We are admonished to speak our own minds concerning it. What earthly reason can any one give for the recording of such a revolting story, except perhaps, to give vent to a sex perversion? Can any element of this story inspire strength of character, or of duty to our fellow-men, or of anything that will elevate the moral life of man?

I do not wish to dwell longer upon this story; but in passing, let me leave this thought with you. Think of a story for a child to read at

Sunday School, or anywhere else, where a woman is of so little worth that she is given to a mob of sensual beasts "to do (to her) what seemeth good unto them," with the consequence that she is abused to death!

Chapter IX.

King David of Israel and His Wives.

We now come to the story of David, King of the Jews, Conqueror of Goliath, Man after God's own heart, and the most infamous character in the long list of reprobates with which the Bible acquaints us.

When I first read the history, or life story, of this man as recorded in the Bible, I was tempted to write exclusively about him, but I realized it would be a task that would prevent the completion of my book and for that reason will leave it for a future time. I assure you he offers fit material for a special study, and after I have recorded those portions which come within the scope of my subject you will not need much additional evidence of his viciousness to convince you of the correctness of my estimate of this malignant rascal, whose character has been extolled from the lips of almost every preacher of every denomination of the western world.

Around the character of this man is woven the fable of his conquest over the giant of the Philistines, Goliath. As children, we were told how David, with his sling, destroyed the giant who was equipped with an armored protection that could withstand an army of Israelites. It is always the negative and destructive things of life that the Bible teaches us to revere; and what makes it so much more pernicious is the hypocritical assurance that "it is the Lord's will."

David was to accomplish great and heroic feats because the Lord was on his side and gave him invisible support.

For pure, unadulterated gibberish concerning the "Lord" and his silly conversations and influences, you are requested to take your Bible in hand, turn to the first book of Samuel, and read the effusions you will find therein. Just as the story of Joseph and his coat of many colors is related to us in our childhood, and arouses our curiosity, and prompts us to become more acquainted with his life, so the story of David and Goliath prompts us to inquire for more details concerning David's life.

It is this instilled interest which we receive in our childhood which makes the character of David such a vicious influence. Especially since, despite his unscrupulousness and despicableness, "God" was ever ready and willing, like a menial servant, not only to protect him, but to give him more power. I do not know of a more pernicious and harmful character study than that of David, King of the Jews, as related in the first and second books of Samuel, as revealed through the "divine word of an Ever-Living God."

Ministers of all denominations plead for another David to lead them in a great spiritual revival. Let us examine the moral side of his life to determine whether or not the people of our day really want another David. I venture to say, were such a character living among us to-day, he would be the object of bitter denunciation and contempt. David's first matrimonial venture is indeed of interest to us, and the method by which he secured his wife is of additional import. Since he had so many wives, the method by which he secured them is of more than ordinary interest. In fact, I might say, that his "courtships" were exceedingly spicy. Debutantes especially should be interested in the amorous adventures of this gallant and debonair Israelite. Previous to the reign of David, Saul was King of the Jews. During his kingship, Saul was quite jealous of David, because the people proclaimed David as "the slayer of ten-thousands" and Saul merely as "the slayer of only thousands."

As the Bible describes this episode so flawlessly let me quote it. Samuel 1, Chapter 18, Verses 6-8.

6. And it came to pass as they came, when David was returned from the slaughter of the Philistine, that the women came out of all cities of Israel, singing and dancing, to meet king Saul, with tabrets, with joy, and with instruments of music.

7. And the women answered one another as they played, and said, Saul hath slain his thousands, and David his ten thousands.

8. And Saul was very wroth, and the saying displeased him; and he said, They have ascribed unto David ten thousands, and to me they have ascribed but thousands: and what can he have more but the kingdom?

The conquering hero returns and receives the plaudits of the multitude. That the King should be jealous of his general, is for the moment not our concern. We are interested in the King's jealousy only as it reveals the method he uses to satisfy his revenge. It may be permissible at this moment to say a word in passing regarding the Bible as a Great War Book. Its pages abound with battles and the devastation wrought by the conquerors is an inspiration to modern war makers. When ministers plead for another David perhaps they want another Savage Commander. Surely the proper place for the Bible is in the War Colleges of belligerent nations.

Killing and murder are related with so little compunction that a continued reading of the Bible cannot help but make one callous to the value of human life. No wonder the Christian countries at war use the Bible as the basis of their national religion and give each soldier a copy while engaged in battle. The spirit of its teachings could not be more accurately followed; its fruits never better revealed.

Samuel 1, Chapter 18, Verses 9-10.

9. And Saul eyed David from that day and forward.

10. And it came to pass on the morrow, that the evil spirit from God came upon Saul, and he prophesied in the midst of the house: and David played with his hand, as at other times: and there was a javelin in Saul's hand.

To digress for a moment. In a conversation recently with a Christian Scientist who maintained that there was "no evil in the world," I replied, by quoting the above verse, which says, "That an evil spirit from God came upon Saul," and I continued by saying, "if there were no evil in the world, what was God doing with it?" There were two answers to my "impertinence." One, that the party was not sufficiently acquainted with the "science" of Christian Science to reply properly to me, and the second, that I was an infidel and would not understand anyway!

But back to David and Saul, whose animosities have arisen to the "boiling point." Saul proceeds to "throw" a little of the "evil spirit" of God at David, as recorded in the following.

Samuel 1, Chapter 18, Verses 11-15.

11. And Saul cast the javelin; for he said, I will smite David even to the wall with it. And David avoided out of his presence twice.

12. And Saul was afraid of David, because the Lord was with him, and was departed from Saul.

13. Therefore Saul removed him from him, and made him his captain over a thousand; and he went out and came in before the people.

14. And David behaved himself wisely in all his ways; and the Lord was with him.

15. Wherefore when Saul saw that he behaved himself very wisely, he was afraid of him.

When "the evil spirit from God" was unable to accomplish any satisfactory results for Saul he proceeds to use more subtle methods. As the next verse reveals the secret of popularity, and as I wish all to be acquainted with this valuable recipe, I will quote it independently.

Samuel 1, Chapter 18, Verse 16.

16. But all Israel and Judah loved David, because he went out and came in before them.

What is meant by "because he went out and came in before them" is more than I can understand. I will leave its interpretation to one who possesses a more spiritual understanding.

Samuel 1, Chapter 18, Verse 17.

17. And Saul said to David, Behold my elder daughter Merab, her will I give thee to wife: only be thou valiant for me, and fight the Lord's battles. For Saul said, Let not mine hand be upon him, but let the hand of the Philistines be upon him.

Evidently the "evil spirit of God" was something of a warning to Saul not to harm David with his own hands, so he conceives the idea of sending him out to do battle, with the hope that the enemy might be successful in killing him. To avoid the suspicion of a deliberate plan, Saul offers his daughter as wife to David and we continue.

Samuel 1, Chapter 18, Verses 18-19.

18. And David said unto Saul, Who am I? and what is my life, or my father's family in Israel, that I should be son in law to the king?

19. But it came to pass at the time when Merab Saul's daughter should have been given to David, that she was given unto Adriel the Meholathite to wife.

The reason Saul's daughter Merab was not given to David is very simple. She was given to Adriel the Meholathite, whoever that gentleman might be. But ah! Saul had another daughter, for if he had not, our story might end here, and just think of the tremendous loss there would have been to the human race

Samuel 1, Chapter 18, Verses 20-21.

20. And Michal Saul's daughter loved David: and they told Saul, and the thing pleased him.

21. And Saul said, I will give him her, that she may be a snare to him, and that the hand of the Philistines may be against him. Wherefore Saul said to David, Thou shalt this day be my son in law in the one of the twain.

So far in our acquaintance with the Bible we have seen a father commit incest with his daughter; give her to a mob of brutal men "to do to her as was good in their eyes," and now we come to a new employment for her: she is used now to be a snare to her husband. Surely a fine outlook for a daughter to look forward to in time of marriage. To be wedded to a man not for love and honor and companionship, but to ensnare him.

Before Saul would give his daughter Michal to David as his wife, he demanded a tribute from him, in the hope that in securing this tribute he would be killed; thus Saul would be relieved of the annoyance of the presence of David and live securely in the possession of his kingdom. The "God-like" attitude of the early Jews to one another is surely compatible with the idea of brotherhood we so anxiously long for to-day.

Samuel 1, Chapter 18, Verses 22-25.

22. And Saul commanded his servants, saying, Commune with David secretly, and say, Behold, the king hath delight in thee, and all his servants love thee: now therefore be the king's son in law.

23. And Saul's servants spake those words in the ears of David. And David said, Seemeth it to you a light thing to be a king's son in law, seeing that I am a poor man, and lightly esteemed?

24. And the servants of Saul told him saying, On this manner spake David.

25. And Saul said, Thus shall ye say to David, The king desireth not any dowry, but a hundred foreskins of the Philistines, to be avenged of the king's enemies. But Saul thought to make David fall by the hand of the Philistines.

Only the writers of the Bible could conceive such a hideous tribute. Not money, not obedience, not the skins of wild animals, but the foreskins of one hundred innocent men! No wonder Saul expected David to be killed in such a perilous undertaking.

David "fell" for Saul's plot and was so overjoyed at the prospect of becoming the King's son-in-law that he unceremoniously doubled the tribute originally demanded by his prospective father-in-law, as we note from the following.

Samuel 1, Chapter 18, Verses 26-30.

26. And when his servants told David these words, it pleased David well to be the king's son in law: and the days were not expired.

27. Wherefore David arose and went, he and his men, and slew of the Philistines two hundred men; and David brought their foreskins, and they gave them in full tale to the king, that he might be the king's son in law. And Saul gave him Michal his daughter to wife.

28. And Saul saw and knew that the Lord was with David, and that Michal Saul's daughter loved him.

29. And Saul was yet the more afraid of David; and Saul became David's enemy continually.

30. Then the princes of the Philistines went forth; and it came to pass, after they went forth, that David behaved himself more wisely than all the servants of Saul; so that his name was much set by.

The devilish means of satisfaction of the early Biblical "heroes" deserve out utmost contempt. Instead of the Bible being preserved as a "sacred volume," its recognition as a history should be strenuously opposed by the Jews as an abomination and insult to their race. The murdering of two hundred men in order to secure their foreskins is but a minor and insignificant event.

As there existed no scruples among the Israelites as to the number of wives a man should have, and as David was one of the glorious leaders, I shall proceed to chronicle the next matrimonial event of this celebrated character.

In recording the event to follow, there is used in the Biblical narrative, as spoken by David, a most insulting expression. It is uttered with all the venom of a rowdy and reveals the coarseness of this type of man. Were our child to use the same expression, as we are about to quote from the Bible, he would be admonished in severe terms never to use such an expression again. It is too coarse a word for even the dictionary to make mention of; even to the extent that it is "not used in polite speech." But why use the dictionary as the criterion of speech, when the Bible is considered the masterpiece of literature?

The time in which this part of the story of David is related transpires just before the death of Saul and the ascendancy of David to the throne as King of the Jews. The intervening events either reveal God as being an imbecile, the Jews as a savage tribe, or the Bible as a monstrous lie. But as we are concerned with the taking of the second wife by David, we cannot digress at this time to expose any other phase of the Bible. To continue, then:

Samuel 1, Chapter 25, Verses 1-2.

And Samuel died; and all the Israelites were gathered together, and lamented him, and buried him in his house at Ramah. And David arose, and went down to the wilderness of Paran.

2. And there was a man in Maon, whose possessions were in Carmel; and the man was very great, and he had three thousand sheep, and a thousand goats: and he was shearing his sheep in Carmel.

That David was the leader of a tribe no better than a gang of bandits, can be seen from what is to follow.

Samuel 1, Chapter 25, Verse 3.

3. Now the name of the man was Nabal, and the name of his wife Abigail; and she was a woman of good understanding, and of a beautiful countenance: but the man was churlish and evil in his doings; and he was of the house of Caleb.

Before proceeding with the narrative, note well what is recorded in the verse above. Here is a man who evidently through hard work and honest labor had accumulated considerable wealth for those days; he also possessed a wife who was "a woman of good understanding, and of a beautiful countenance." In what respect and why he was "churlish and evil in his doings" is not recorded. That he was more unprincipled or unscrupulous than David, is hardly conceivable.

Samuel 1, Chapter 25, Verses 4-8.

4. And David heard in the wilderness that Nabal did shear his sheep.

5. And David sent out ten young men, and David said unto the young men, Get you up to Carmel, and go to Nabal, and greet him in my name:

6. And thus shall ye say to him that liveth in prosperity. Peace be both to thee, and peace be to thine house, and peace be unto all that thou hast.

7. And now I have heard that thou hast shearers: now thy shepherds which were with us, we hurt them not, neither was there aught missing unto them, all the while they were in Carmel.

8. Ask thy young men, and they will shew thee. Wherefore let the young men find favour in thine eyes; for we come in a good day: give: I pray thee, whatsoever cometh to thine hand unto thy servants, and to thy son David.

For downright maliciousness you will have to go a long way to encounter another similar instance of gaining tribute. In other words, David practiced a method of blackmail. "Pay me not to commit trespass upon your property" is in substance what David demanded. A fine code of ethics does this story of the Bible teach!

Samuel 1, Chapter 25, Verse 9.

9. And when David's young men came, they spake to Nabal according to all those words into the name of David, and ceased.

Here is a difficult situation. Here is an honest man with valuable possessions approached by messengers of an arch bandit and blackmailer demanding tribute for immunity from pillage. What would any courageous man maintain in the face of such an outrageous proposal. To-day we would notify the police, but unfortunately at that time the institution of law and government was not so far advanced. Our present code is, "millions for defense, but not one cent for tribute." No doubt Nabal thought of the same thing, and rightly too; for he answers David's men as follows.

Samuel 1, Chapter 25, Verses 10-11.

10. And Nabal answered David's servants, and said, Who is David? and who is the son of Jesse? there be many servants nowadays that break away every man from his master.

11. Shall I then take my bread, and my water, and my flesh that I have killed for my shearers, and give it unto men, whom I know not whence they be?

Was there ever a more unjust demand and was there ever a more justified refusal than the utterance just recorded of Nabal? Nabal was not only justified in what he said; it was his duty as a man to refuse to acquiesce to the banditry of David. The following is of deep significance and I bid you to read carefully.

Samuel 1, Chapter 25, Verses 12-13.

12. So David's young men turned their way, and went again, and came and told him all those sayings.

13. And David said unto his men, Gird ye on every man his sword. And they girded on every man his sword; and David also girded on his sword; and there went up after David about four hundred men; and two hundred abode by the stuff.

Think of the damnable character of a person who will destroy an innocent man and rob him of his belongings because of a justified refusal!

But why think about the character of the Biblical leaders?

Do you expect a thief to honor the code of honesty?

Do you expect a murderer to hold human life sacred?

Do you expect the profligate to respect the virtuous?

Then expect none of these things from any of the characters of the Bible. They are too "divine" for that. We must look to ungodly human beings to possess such virtues.

Samuel 1, Chapter 25, Verses 14-17.

14. But one of the young men told Abigail, Nabal's wife, saying, Behold, David sent messengers out of the wilderness to salute our master; and he railed on them.

15. But the men were very good unto us, and we were not hurt, neither missed we any thing, as long as we were conversant with them, when we were in the fields.

16. They were a wall unto us both by night and day, all the while we were with them keeping the sheep.

17. Now therefore know and consider what thou wilt do; for evil is determined against our master, and against all his household: for he is such a son of Belial, that a man cannot speak to him.

18. Then Abigail made haste, and took two hundred loaves, and two bottles of wine, and five sheep ready dressed, and five measures of parched corn, and a hundred clusters of raisins, and two hundred cakes of figs, and laid them on asses.

19. And she said unto her servants, Go on before me; behold, I come after you. But she told not her husband Nabal.

20. And it was so, as she rode on the ass, that she came down by the covert of the hill, and, behold, David and his men came down against her; and she met them.

21. Now David had said, Surely in vain have I kept all that this fellow hath in the wilderness, so that nothing was missed of all that pertained unto him: and he hath requited me evil for good.

So much for the tribute, and now let us see what would have happened if the tribute was not forthcoming. In the verse to follow appears, as I stated before, the most ribald expression that has ever appeared in any book of general circulation. It may be all right for the Bible to make mention of this expression, but I do not want to give currency to it.

Samuel 1, Chapter 25, Verse 22.

22. So and more also do God unto the enemies of David, if I leave of all that pertain to him by the morning light any that ... against the wall.

Surely there is a perverted cunning in the manner of describing men as stated in the last verse. To use this expression but once is not sufficient, and as the Bible wishes to impress this elevating detail upon our minds it is used again in a less ambiguous sentence after Abigail prostrates herself before David in supplication and thanks him for witholding his vengeance. As it is necessary to quote this scene to continue the story, I will proceed.

Samuel 1, Chapter 25, Verses 23-34.

23. And when Abigail saw David, she hasted, and lighted off the ass, and fell before David on her face, and bowed herself to the ground.

24. And fell at his feet, and said, Upon me, my lord, upon me let this iniquity be: and let thine handmaid, I pray thee, speak in thine audience, and hear the words of thine handmaid.

25. Let not my lord, I pray thee, regard this man of Belial, even Nabal: for as his name is, so is he; Nabal is his name, and folly is with him: but I thine handmaid saw not the young men of my lord, whom thou didst send.

26. Now therefore, my lord, as the Lord liveth, and As thy soul liveth, seeing the Lord hath withholden thee from coming to shed blood, and from avenging thyself with thine own hand, now let thine enemies, and they that seek evil to my lord, be as Nabal.

27. And now this blessing which thine handmaid hath brought unto my lord, let it even be given unto the young men that follow my lord.

28. I pray thee, forgive the trespass of thine handmaid: for the Lord will certainly make my lord a sure house; because my lord fighteth the battles of the Lord, and evil hath not been found in thee all thy days.

29. Yet a man is risen to pursue thee, and to seek thy soul: but the soul of my lord shall be bound in the bundle of life with the Lord thy God; and the souls of thine enemies, them shall he sling out, as out of the middle of a sling.

30. And it shall come to pass, when the Lord shall have done to my lord according to all the good that he hath spoken concerning thee, and shall have appointed thee ruler over Israel;

31. That this shall be no grief unto thee, nor offence of heart unto my lord, either that thou hast shed blood causeless, or that my lord hath avenged himself: but when the Lord shall have dealt well with my lord, then remember thine handmaid.

32. And David said to Abigail, Blessed be the Lord God of Israel, which sent thee this day to meet me:

33. And blessed he thy advice, and blessed be thou, which hast kept me this day from coming to shed blood, and from avenging myself with mine own hand.

34. For in very deed as the Lord God of Israel liveth, which hath kept me back from hurting thee, except thou hadst hasted and come to meet

me, surely there had not been left unto Nabal by the morning light any that ... against the wall.

What damnable hypocrisy and all that man abhors in life is contained in the above quotation. If the "Lord God of Israel" prompts men to be so fiendish, then the sooner we get rid of such a being, the better off we will be.

Samuel 1, Chapter 25, Verse 35.

35. So David received of her hand that which she had brought him, and said unto her, Go up in peace to thine house; see, I have hearkened to thy voice, and have accepted thy person.

David has been satisfied. Whether it was the tribute that Abigail brought him or the acceptance of "thy person" which appeased his anger we are not told. I am inclined to think it was the latter, as subsequent events would lead one to believe.

Samuel 1, Chapter 25, Verses 36-38.

36. And Abigail came to Nabal; and, behold, he held a feast in his house, like the feast of a king; and Nabal's heart was merry within him, for he was very drunken: wherefore she told him nothing, less or more, until the morning light.

37. But it came to pass in the morning, when the wine was gone out of Nabal, and his wife had told him these things, that his heart died within him, and he became as a stone.

38. And it came to pass about ten days after, that the Lord smote Nabal, that he died.

What could have suited David better? Upon being informed of the tragic occurrence he "sent and communed with Abigail, to take her to him to wife."

Samuel 1, Chapter 25, Verses 39-42.

39. And when David heard that Nabal was dead, he said, Blessed be the Lord, that hath pleaded the cause of my reproach from the hand of Nabal, and hath kept his servant from evil: for the Lord hath returned the wickedness of Nabal upon his own head. And David sent and communed with Abigail, to take her to him to wife.

40. And when the servants of David were come to Abigail to Carmel, they spake unto her, saying, David sent us unto thee, to take thee to him to wife.

41. And she arose, and bowed herself on her face to the earth, and said, Behold, let thine handmaid be a servant to wash the feet of the servants of my lord.

42. And Abigail hasted, and arose, and rode upon an ass, with five damsels of hers that went after her; and she went after the messengers of David, and became his wife.

Abigail was so overjoyed at becoming the wife of David that, to show her dutifulness, she was ready and willing to be a servant to wash the feet of the servants of her lord. But, to David, a wife evidently meant another servant, for in the following verse, without the slightest indication that he was "in the market" he takes another wife.

Samuel 1, Chapter 25, Verse 43.

43. David also took Ahinoam of Jezreel; and they were also both of them his wives.

Certainly our moralists have reason to be indebted to the Bible for the inculcation of the high principles enunciated regarding the institution of marriage.

Before proceeding with the next event in the life of David, I want to say a word regarding the expression used in this narrative. Were a book written containing such a reference as expressed in verse 34, what would be your opinion of it? Do you think we would revere the author as "divinely inspired" and hold sacred the book as the "Word of God"?

In a recent conviction of the producers of a play, the Court of General Sessions of the City of New York, held that "the moral ending of a play does not justify presentation of scenes which shock public sense of decency."[6]

In the story just related about David there is not only no moral ending, but a distinctly *immoral* one and there are *numerous presentations which shock public sense of decency.* By the wildest stretch of the imagination I cannot understand what prompts public officials to put the Bible in our public schools. What right has the government, in view of the exposure already made, to exempt churches from taxation where the Bible is being expounded as the Word of God? Surely hypocrisy added to filth is not deserving of this favoritism. How much more will it be necessary to record, before the people awaken to the seriousness of the Bible's teachings in relation to morality?

As for King David, this is merely an incident in his life. What is to follow is even more repulsive. It is impossible to relate in detail the

---

[6] *The New York Sun,* December 16, 1924.

events which take place in the life of David until the time of his next licentious episode; and for that reason his brutal commands, his deception by proclaiming peace unto a nation and then pillaging that nation must be referred directly to the Bible. The ruthless devastation wrought upon defenseless people must likewise be left unrecorded. The taking of women of a conquered province for the lust of his men must also be passed without comment. And yet the preachers have the audacity to say that the world is looking for another leader like David!

During the events mentioned above we find David was not satisfied with only three wives, and by way of diversion took unto himself several more, even while engaged in battle, as we learn from the following.

Samuel 2, Chapter 3, Verses 2-5.

2. And unto David were sons born in Hebron: and his firstborn was Amnon, of Ahinoam the Jezreelitess;

3. And his second, Chileab, of Abigail the wife of Nabal the Carmelite; and the third, Absalom the son of Maacah the daughter of Talmai king of Geshur;

4. And the fourth, Adonijah the son of Haggith, and the fifth, Shephatiah the son of Abital;

5. And the sixth, Ithream, by Eglah David's wife. These were born to David in Hebron.

So far, if I have not been inaccurate in my calculations, David has taken unto his bosom seven wives. But what is a mere seven wives to a man like David? The circumstances surrounding the "taking" of the above mentioned wives are not recorded and therefore we cannot relate in detail the romantic courtship attending each marriage. Despite the fact that he found favor in his six other wives, David returns to his original mate, for whom, if you remember, he gave two hundred foreskins of the Philistines, and his entrance and approach to her is worth recording.

Samuel 2, Chapter 6, Verse 20.

20. Then David returned to bless his household. And Michal the daughter of Saul came out to meet David, and said, How glorious was the king of Israel to day, who uncovered himself to day in the eyes of the handmaids of his servants, as one of the vain fellows shamelessly uncovereth himself!

What a nice scene this must have been. I wonder what passion, or rather insanity obsessed David to so shamelessly uncover himself! I wonder what the handmaids and servants thought of this "glorious man of God." Were they to follow his example? Or was David the first of that religious sect which practices the custom of living in complete nakedness?

Samuel 2, Chapter 6, Verse 21.

21. And David said unto Michal, It was before the Lord, which chose me before thy father, and before all his house, to appoint me ruler over the people of the Lord, over Israel; therefore will I play before the Lord.

Nakedness of course is not a crime, yet it is not particularly desirable in our present mode of living and standard of morals. Even bathing suits, suitable for swimming, are objected to by the very ones who preach from the Bible and uphold the action of David, and yet admonish the people to be more moral!

Samuel 2, Chapter 6, Verses 22-23.

22. And I will yet be more vile than thus and will be base in mine own sight: and of the maidservants which thou hast spoken of, of them shall I be had in honour.

23. Therefore Michal the daughter of Saul had no child unto the day of her death.

David warns us he *"will yet be more vile than thus,"* so let us be prepared for what is to follow. Why Michal should be penalized with sterility for her reprimand to David the "Lord only knows," for certainly we approve of her action.

But there is a contradiction in the above statement, for Michal did bear children. The Bible itself says, Samuel 2, Chapter 21, Verse 8, "and the five sons of Michal, the daughter of Saul, whom she brought up from Adriel the son of Barzillai the Metholathite." Perhaps Michal herself was practicing a bit of adultery on the side, while David was *taking* his other wives, but why the Lord knew nothing about it I cannot say.

Before continuing to the next phase of this story it will not be out of place, I hope, to record an instance or two which took place in the intervening time. David has now become the King of the Jews and with the Lord's help has grown great as we find in Samuel 2, Chapter 5, Verses 10-12.

10. And David went on, and grew great, and the Lord God of hosts was with him.

11. And Hiram king of Tyre sent messengers to David, and cedar trees, and carpenters, and masons: and they built David a house.

12. And David perceived that the Lord had established him king over Israel, and that he had exalted his kingdom for his people Israel's sake.

But to David more power meant more wives. Samuel 2, Chapter 5, Verses 13-16.

13. And David took him more concubines and wives out of Jerusalem, after he was come from Hebron: and there were yet sons and daughters born to David.

14. And these be the names of those that were born unto him in Jerusalem; Shammuah, and Shobab, and Nathan, and Solomon,

15. Ibhar also, and Elishua, and Nepheg, and Japhia,

16. And Elishama, and Eliada, and Eliphalet.

As this text does not mention the exact number of wives which David took after he was come from Hebron we must discontinue the count. Since the word "wives" is plural and means more than one we must conclude, figuring the very minimum, David has at least nine wives and truly an infinite number of concubines, as we have absolutely no record of the number of those poor creatures he possessed. I ask you to note the name of one of his sons as mentioned in the 14th verse quoted above. Is this the same Solomon who ascended the throne of David after his father's death? Or did David have two sons by the name of Solomon. For how could David have a son by a woman before he knew her? Or is this another instance of the utter stupidity, and unreliableness of the Bible, its writers and translators? What is to follow is so ludicrous I cannot resist quoting it to you.

Samuel 2, Chapter 5, Verses 17-19.

17. But when the Philistines heard that they had anointed David king over Israel, all the Philistines came up to seek David; and David heard of it, and went down to the hold.

18. The Philistines also came and spread themselves in the valley of Rephaim.

19. And David inquired of the Lord, saying, Shall I go up to the Philistines? wilt thou deliver them into mine hand? And the Lord said unto David, Go up: for I will doubtless deliver the Philistines into thine hand.

Please read again the verse just quoted. David asks the Lord what he should do regarding the war-like maneuvers of the Philistines and the Lord speaks to David as follows: "For I will doubtless deliver the Philistines into thine hands." Can you imagine God saying he would *doubtless* do a certain thing? The Bible is not only ludicrous in its expressions, but is silly and foolish as well.

We now come to the most despicable episode in the life of this Jewish scoundrel. It alone is sufficient to brand with the mark of infamy the character responsible for the crime. And yet it is but an ordinary incident in the life of David, a lark, so to speak, in the life of this "man of God." But to us poor mortals it is a story of a different color. To us it reveals a character that we judge to be an abomination. Were such an unscrupulous man living to-day openly committing such a vile deed, our condemnation would resound the world over; and instead of applying the title "man of God" to such a scoundrel, we would more properly refer to him in language befitting his rascality. Since David *was* a man of God, and since the Bible is God's Holy Word, we will proceed with the story.

Samuel 2, Chapter 11, Verses 1-2.

And it came to pass, after the year was expired, at the time when kings go forth to battle, that David sent Joab, and his servants with him, and all Israel; and they destroyed the children of Ammon, and besieged Rabbah. But David tarried still at Jerusalem.

2. And it came to pass in an evening tide, that David arose from off his bed, and walked upon the roof of the king's house: and from the roof he saw a woman washing herself; and the woman was very beautiful to look upon.

It may be of interest here to mention the fact, that in the days of the great religious leaders -- men who had either seen or spoken to God -- the abodes in which they lived did not have the conveniences of the modern home. Gas and electric light were not only unknown, but had such "miracles" even been suggested a charge of witchcraft would have followed the proposal. Household plumbing and that essential, the bathtub, were improvements these God-inspired men were totally ignorant of. They were "inspired" with higher ideals than those which make for comfort and happiness of the family. They were inspired with warfare, deception, rape and banditry. These improvements came from men who did not boast of any relation with God. They were concerned with peace, the cultivation of their soil and the uplift of the community. For following these pursuits and endeavoring to improve the conditions under which they lived, these people were termed by such fiendish characters as David and his like as pagans, infidels and heretics.

But let us go back to our story where the great King David -- we should judge it to be in the twilight of evening, in the balmy month of June -- walked upon the roof of his house and lo and behold, saw a woman washing herself. A closer observation revealed the woman -- in her nakedness -- as being very beautiful. As there are more details to the story we will let the Bible whisper them to us.

Samuel 2, Chapter 11, Verses 34.

3. And David sent and inquired after the woman. And one said, Is not this Bath-sheba, the daughter of Eliam, the wife of Uriah the Hittite?

4. And David sent messengers, and took her; and she came in unto him, and he lay with her; for she was purified from her uncleanness: and she returned unto her house.

One thing about David; he certainly lost no time in the satisfaction of his lustful desires. What a perfect Biblical character he is. No romance, no wooing on a moonlight night, no fervent manifestations of passionate love; just brutal sexual satisfaction. Aye, even a parody upon prostitution. Not a single line to give a redeeming color to this brutal case of adultery. "And David sent messengers, and took her; and she came in unto him, and he lay with her." As cold-blooded as it is possible to be.

It is not a difficult task to understand what a pernicious influence the Bible exerts upon the world when such a story as this is one of its prominent features. Why, the very conditions under which the Biblical characters lived, and the time and place of the narratives, is sufficient to discredit the Bible as a cultural guide. And the struggle to free mankind from the influence of those barbaric times is constantly interfered with by the Bible and its multitude of deluded supporters and defenders. Before passing to the next event of this episode, I wish to record a thought which has just occurred to me.

Is it possible, because of the circumstances surrounding the event by which David observed Bath-sheba, that she was given her name? Perhaps in her girlhood she was known only as "Sheba," but since David observed her taking a bath she was renamed "Bath-sheba" or "Sheba, the maid of the Bath." I consider this thought well founded and at the same time deserving of mention. I refer it for investigation to those devout Biblical scholars who think it more sacred to read the Bible from morning to night than to do anything useful in the world. But let us see what has happened to Bath-sheba after David "lay with her."

Samuel 2, Chapter 11, Verse 5.

5. And the woman conceived, and sent and told David, and said, I am with child.

Well, what do you expect? What generally results from forbidden sex relation? David was not as considerate as Onan. The question of preventing conception did not enter his mind. Nevertheless, here is an opportunity for David to show his manhood, and at the same time an example of chivalry which would add credit and lustre to his name, and perhaps atone for his dastardly act.

Samuel 2, Chapter 11, Verses 6-11.

6. And David sent to Joab, saying, Send me Uriah the Hittite. And Joab sent Uriah to David.

7. And when Uriah was come unto him, David demanded of him how Joab did, and how the people did, and how the war prospered.

8. And David said to Uriah, Go down to thy house, and wash thy feet. And Uriah departed out of the king's house, and there followed him a mess of meat from the king.

9. But Uriah slept at the door of the king's house with all the servants of his lord, and went not down to his house.

10. And when they had told David, saying, Uriah went not down unto his house, David said unto Uriah, Camest thou not from thy journey? why then didst thou not go down unto thine house?

11. And Uriah said unto David, The ark, and Israel, and Judah, abide in tents; and my lord Joab, and the servants of my lord, are encamped in the open fields; shall I then go into mine house, to eat and to drink, and to lie with my wife? as thou livest, and as thy soul liveth, I will not do this thing.

The words of a true soldier. So loyal was this man Uriah to his duty, he refused on a leave of absence, to go to his own home, enjoy its comforts, and spend the night in the company of his wife, who was, according to the Bible, very beautiful. He preferred to gird himself so as to face more stoically the hardships which he would naturally encounter in the performance of his duty as a soldier. He avoided the temptation of the irresistible desire which he knew would result while in the company of his beautiful wife. He preferred to stand ready to do service to his country and uphold allegiance to his oath. What a pitiable exposure this incident makes of the leaders and makers of war. While men are fighting for their country and fatherland, these securely protected leaders, rulers, and kings find sport with the wives of their loyal subjects.

What reward does David give Uriah for such loyalty? What amends does he make for the seduction of his beautiful wife? More pertinent than anything I might say to impeach the character of David is the following as it consecutively appears in the Bible.

Samuel 2, Chapter 11, Verses 12-15.

12. And David said to Uriah, Tarry here to-day also, and to-morrow I will let thee depart. So Uriah abode in Jerusalem that day, and the morrow.

13. And when David had called him, he did eat and drink before him; and he made him drunk: and at even he went out to lie on his bed with the servants of his lord, but went not down to his house.

14. And it came to pass in the morning, that David wrote a letter to Joab, and sent it by the hand of Uriah.

15. And he wrote in the letter, saying, Set ye Uriah in the forefront of the hottest battle, and retire ye from him, that he may be smitten, and die.

The medal of honor that David gave Uriah for his loyalty and duty as a soldier was his own death warrant. "Set ye Uriah in the forefront of the hottest battle, and retire ye from him, that he may be smitten and die." This is the reward and compensation which Uriah received from the man who had seduced his wife.

This is the chivalry of David, that wonderful Biblical character and leader of the Jews. Shame, shame and everlasting disgrace is such a personage among men; he is anathema. If the Jews take pride in the personage of David, then what do they condemn in a fiend?

And now, if you will let me depart for a moment from the continuity of this story I will demonstrate to you by an actual case, the pernicious influence the Bible, and particularly the story of David, has upon the minds of men and the damnable hypocrisy which follows in its wake.

On Monday, September 22, 1924, in all the newspapers of that day, the horrible and shocking news was sent broadcast that the Reverend Lawrence M. Hight, Methodist minister of Ina, Illinois, had confessed to a diabolical double murder -- that of his loyal and dutiful wife, the mother of his children, and also the husband of his paramour.

If David is "a man after God's own heart," and to emulate David is the surest path to eternal glory, it is no small wonder then that such a conviction not only justifies but actually prompts murder. And did the Reverend Mr. Hight fashion his life after that of David? David wanted Bath-sheba, and so he sent Uriah, her husband, to the forefront of the hottest battle, -- that he may be smitten and die: and similarly, Hight "cast his eyes" upon Mrs. Sweeten, the wife of one of his parishioners and, like David, "sent for her, and he lay with her." He also bought some arsenic poison, which was afterwards administered to her husband.

The New York Sunday American, commenting upon the bold effrontery of this scoundrel, in a full-page feature story, in bold type, says:

Preached the Funeral Sermon
of the Man He Murdered

With pretended grief the Rev. Mr. Hight eulogized his victim's worthy character and wondered why the Almighty had called him to the world beyond. Standing at the head of the flower-decked coffin of the man whose death he had arranged and while the widow, the clergyman's sweetheart, sat beside the casket with her three fatherless boys, the Rev. Mr. Hight preached his hypocritical sermon, which is now recalled with bitter indignation by those who were present.

Although it was unnecessary for David to be rid of his wife (or wives) to take another man's wife, it was necessary for Hight to be free of his, that he might more fully enjoy his "Bath-sheba," and so under the pretense of "ministering to his wife," while she lay ill, pleading for some help, he cold-bloodedly and with murderous intent put arsenic in her coffee, and she died in writhing agony. On a previous occasion, it has now been unearthed, a high-school girl, a pretty organist and member of his flock, died under similar circumstances.

Did Hight think he could commit murder with the same immunity as David? Fortunately the laws of this country are not founded upon the Bible, and this disciple of God is now serving a term of life imprisonment for his "David-like" crime.

Let us pick up the thread of our story and continue with the narrative of the book "blessed with divine inspiration."

Samuel 2, Chapter 11, Verses 16-21.

16. And it came to pass, when Joab observed the city, that he assigned Uriah unto a place where he knew that valiant men were.

17. And the men of the city went out, and fought with Joab; and there fell some of the people of the servants of David; and Uriah the Hittite died also.

18. Then Joab sent and told David all the things concerning the war;

19. And charged the messenger, saying, When thou hast made an end of telling the matters of the war unto the king,

20. And if so be that the king's wrath arise, and he say unto thee, Wherefore approached ye so nigh unto the city when ye did fight? knew ye not that they would shoot from the wall?

21. Who smote Abimelech the son of Jerubbesheth? did not a woman cast a piece of a millstone upon him from the wall, that he died in Thebez? why went ye nigh the wall? then say thou, Thy servant Uriah the Hittite is dead also.

That human life was held valueless by these monsters is self-evident from the above verses. And so diabolical was this cunning, and so anxious were David's lieutenants to please him that hundreds of innocent men were slaughtered that Uriah might die also. How David censured his men for being so unnecessarily murderous follows.

Samuel 2, Chapter 11, Verses 22-25.

22. So the messenger went, and came and shewed David all that Joab had sent him for.

23. And the messenger said unto David, Surely the men prevailed against us, and came out unto us into the field, and we were upon them even unto the entering of the gate.

24. And the shooters shot from off the wall upon thy servants; and some of the king's servants be dead, and thy servant Uriah the Hittite is dead also.

25. Then David said unto the messenger, Thus shalt thou say unto Joab, Let not this thing displease thee, for the sword devoureth one as well as another: make thy battle more strong against the city, and overthrow it: and encourage thou him.

Now that Uriah is dead and no longer an obstacle to the complete fulfillment of David's desire for Bath-sheba, we will let the Bible reveal to us the libidinous details of this episode.

Samuel 2, Chapter 11, Verses 26-27.

26. And when the wife of Uriah heard that Uriah her husband was dead, she mourned for her husband.

27. And when the mourning was past, David sent and fetched her to his house, and she became his wife, and bare him a son. But the thing that David had done displeased the Lord.

So much for the actual record of this foul act.

After accomplishing his ends with diabolical cunning, and Uriah dead, "David sent and fetched Bath-sheba to his house, and she became his wife, and bare him a son." Under the circumstances, Bath-sheba should have considered herself lucky to have had David marry her. The general rule of the Biblical characters is that she would have merely become one of his "women," or as the Bible would say, "concubines." What can one say in commenting upon such a story? Words are inadequate to express properly our feelings. And yet David, because of his deeply religious convictions, is looked upon as an ideal example for our youths. If religious convictions produce such a man as David, then, by all means, the sooner we do away with religion and its mania, the sooner we will be able to attain that high moral standard which the world has set as its goal.

Would you consider the character of David the proper example for your son to follow?

Would you consider the story just related as being conducive to elevate the the moral standard of your children?

With the knowledge of the infamous character of David, would you propose him as being a man fashioned after the heart of God?

What would be your opinion of a God who selected such a man as David to be his prototype?

Yes, I would consider the reading of such a story with the admonition that such a character pictures the loathsomeness and degradation which we should struggle to avoid. But no! The Bible is the Holy Word of an Ever-Existing God and every word carries divine inspiration! Not a single question must be raised against it. Just think of it! The mind of a child is imbued with the thought that this book -- the Bible -- is the Holy of Holies and must be ever held in reverence. Do you wonder at the terrible harm inflicted upon a child when this trash of the Bible is forced upon him as Divine Truth?

And that it must be accepted even with his life as such! And that the book is so sacred, that he must pick it up and kiss it when it falls to the floor!

There is reason enough why the mentality of the world has lagged so miserably behind in the march of progress. Instead of the Bible's being forced upon the people as "divine truth," it should be looked upon as a record of the barbarous acts of long ago when the human race was groping for a path of light in the darkness of ignorance and superstition and savagery.

"But the thing that David had done displeased the Lord," if you remember, and the dastardly crime is brought home to him in the parable of the ewe lamb. And as the story is related to him, and the monstrous crime unfolded, and he perceives the cruel injustice perpetrated, "David's anger was greatly kindled against the man," and he says, "as the Lord liveth, the man that hath done this thing shall surely die." When the grim truth is brought home to him that "Thou art the man," what happened? The "liveth" Lord steps into the scene, and proceeds to inflict punishment for the deed. What a wonderful opportunity for the Lord to reveal a sample of his divine justice that we poor mortals may follow. Let me not tell in my own words what this punishment was that the Lord was to inflict upon David whom he had so lavishly endowed with wealth and power. The Bible tells it in such a way that it deserves to speak for itself.

Samuel 2, Chapter 12, Verses 11-12.

11. Thus saith the Lord, Behold, I will raise up evil against thee out of thine own house, and I will take thy wives before thine eyes, and give them unto thy neighbour, and he shall lie with thy wives in the sight of this sun.

12 For thou didst it secretly: but I will do this thing before all Israel, and before the sun.

Surely the world should listen when the Lord speaks. And what does he say? Does he tell David that for his crime he will take from him his kingdom, his wealth and his power? No. He tells David that for his crime he will take his wives from him, and give them to his neighbor, "and he shall lie with them in the sight of this sun", so all may see it, and that David may suffer humiliation for his deed.

Divine Justice, mingled with a delicate and edifying situation! What a most interesting scene this must have been! Performing such an act in broad daylight as a punishment for a hellish crime !

And now a thought about David's poor wives. What did they do to merit such a disgrace? They did not become his wives willingly; David, with the help of God, took them. And if they did willingly choose their wifehood, what difference would that make? Why should they be made to suffer such humiliation with other men before the eyes of all the people for a crime committed by their husband. If God is just, why didn't he punish David himself for the crime he committed?

God's action is not only abhorrent to our sense of justice, but his action puts woman in a position beneath that of the promiscuous dog. If this is a sample of divine justice, the sooner we get rid of God, the sooner real justice will prevail. But all this talk about what the Lord intended to do to David was mere spoofing, for we read in the next verse:

Samuel 2, Chapter 12, Verse 13.

13. And David said unto Nathan, I have sinned against the Lord. And Nathan said unto David, The Lord also hath put away thy sin; thou shalt not die.

What can we say of such an example of justice? David merely made a confession, like the rites practiced in the Catholic church, and he was absolved of his sin. The narrative does not make mention of any contribution, so I presume another method was in vogue in those days to "satisfy the Lord." Nowadays the contribution box is a very essential part of the "absolution."

Is this method of repentance conducive to the development of high moral character? Can a person "commit any crime on the calendar," and surely David did, and then say, "I have sinned against the Lord" (by the way this is what Hight said when he was apprehended) and all is forgiven and the punishment stayed? Is this where the Catholic church got one of its most profitable principles? What do you think of such a method; of such a travesty of the holy principle of right; of such a "covering up" for such a dastardly crime?

David's punishment is very similar to that of Judah in his illicit relations with his daughter-in-law, Tamar. You remember when Judah was informed that Tamar, his daughter-in-law, was with child by whoredom, he cried, "Bring her forth that she may be burnt," and when he was confronted with the evidence showing by whom she was with child, and he recognized it as belonging to him, he punished himself to the extent that he "knew her again no more."

In beginning my task of writing this book I did not think I would encounter such distasteful episodes. I feel as if I have already recounted a sufficient amount of obnoxious scenes from the Bible to alone condemn it before the world; but I cannot stop now. No matter how distasteful my task becomes I believe my efforts in bringing to light just what the Bible *actually* contains, will more than repay the effort I put into the work. If I can convince the people that the Bible is not the Holy book they were taught to believe it is, I will consider my work well repaid. If I can bring the truth of the Bible to the attention of our Government officials and have them withdraw the Government sanction and support of it, my work will be productive of great benefit and I will feel more than satisfied with such a recompense.

We have not concluded all there is to say about David, although enough has been recorded to bring the blush of shame to a multitude of libertines. The climax of his life is very fitting and proper and we will proceed to it, despite the fact "that as the Lord liveth this man would surely die." What would you expect would be the final act of the man whose wickedness we have just related? What would be the general attitude of most men who had lived a most profligate life and knew that the end was at hand? What moral ending would you expect to find, as a final act of David's life, in a book that for nearly two thousand years has been sacredly worshipped as the infallible Word of God? Surely here is an opportunity to give to the world an example of a repentent soul. Truly a message that one could call divine. But it is the following episode which concludes the life of "David the son of Jesse, and the man who was raised up on high, the anointed of the God of Jacob, and the sweetest psalmist of Israel."[7] What a mockery!

The delectable scene follows.

The First Book of Kings, Chapter 1, Verse 1.

---

[7] Samuel 2, Chapter 23, Verse 1.

Now king David was old and stricken in years; and they covered him with clothes, but he gat no heat.

Now if you think David was covered with clothes merely for the purpose of keeping his body warm, you are greatly mistaken and I am surprised at your ignorance. It was for an altogether different purpose that efforts were made to give him heat, as the following verse reveals.

The First Book of Kings, Chapter 1, Verse 2.

2. Wherefore his servants said unto him, Let there be sought for my lord the king a young virgin: and let her stand before the king, and let her cherish him, and let her lie in thy bosom, that my lord the king may get heat.

Of all of David's wives and concubines none were sought to arouse within his breast a final passionate response. The beautiful Bath-sheba has lost her charm and the multitude of his other women were as stale bread. Perhaps the delicacy of the untouched soft skin of a young virgin was necessary to arouse that spark of sexual desire to overcome the harrowing impotence in this Biblical Lothario. Certainly the method selected to revive his "heat" was a most delightful one, as recorded in the following.

The First Book of Kings, Chapter 1, Verses 3-4.

3. So they sought for a fair damsel throughout all the coasts of Israel, and found Abishag a Shunammite, and brought her to the king.

4 And the damsel was very fair, and cherished the hug, and ministered to him: but the king knew her not.

What a delicate mission the servants of David undertook, in examining all the young girls "throughout all the coasts of Israel" to determine their virginity and pick out the most beautiful one. I wonder if there were a scramble by all the young ladies to submit to the scrutinizing examination? Or rather was there a protest against such an abominable undertaking?

But the more we inquire into the social conditions of the people of the Biblical narratives the more we are convinced that the less said the better. So after the examination of the young girls "throughout all the coasts of Israel," a damsel "very fair" was found; and she "cherished the king, and ministered to him: but the king knew her not." Let us reflect for a moment on what is recorded in the verses just quoted.

Abishag, this beautiful young virgin, "cherished and ministered" to David. Now what do the narrators mean by that? What an elevating and inspiring scene this must have been. What a situation it presented!

91

What a conundrum it must be to a clergyman to explain this event of David's life to his congregation.

All the efforts of the beautiful young virgin seem to have been of no avail; even to that of "lying in his bosom." If David was unable to respond to the caresses of a beautiful young damsel, "that had not known man," as the Bible would say, then surely his poignancy must have been indeed great. Impotence to David was worse than death, and even the Lord offered no help to David in his plight.

That Abishag "ministered" to David for a considerable time and that David made heroic efforts to "gat" heat that he may "know her," can be judged from the quotation of verses 15 and 16 of the same chapter. While Abishag was ministering to David, Nathan, the prophet, was entreating Bath-sheba to intervene with David before he died that Solomon should inherit the throne, for news had just been brought to them that another son by another wife had set up a throne and had proclaimed himself King of Israel.

That Bath-sheba was aware that a young virgin was ministering to her husband seems quite evident also from the following.

The First Book of Kings, Chapter 1, Verses 5-16.

5. Then Adonijah the son of Haggith exalted himself, saying, I will be king: and he prepared him chariots and horsemen, and fifty men to run before him.

6. And his father had not displeased him at any time in saying, Why hast thou done so? and he also was a very goodly man; and his mother bare him after Absalom.

7. And he conferred with Joab the son of Zeruiah, and with Abiathar the priest: and they following Adonijah helped him.

8. But Zadok the priest, and Benaiah the son of Jehoiada, and Nathan the prophet, and Shimei, and Rei, and the mighty men which belonged to David, were not with Adonijah.

9. And Adonijah slew sheep and oxen and fat cattle by the stone of Zoheleth, which is by Enrogel, and called all his brethren the king's sons, and all the men of Judah the king's servant:

10. But Nathan the prophet, and Benaiah, and the mighty men, and Solomon his brother, he called not.

11. Wherefore Nathan spake unto Bath-sheba the mother of Solomon, saying, Hast thou not heard that Adonijah the son of Haggith doth reign, and David our lord knoweth it not?

12. Now therefore come, let me, I pray thee, give thee counsel, that thou mayest save thine own life, and the life of thy son Solomon.

13 Go and get thee in unto king David, and say unto him, Didst not thou, my lord, O king, swear unto thine handmaid, saying, Assuredly Solomon thy son shall reign after me, and he shall sit upon my throne? why then doth Adonijah reign?

14. Behold, while thou yet talkest there with the king, I also will come in after thee, and confirm thy words.

15. And Bath-sheba went in unto the king into the chamber: and the king was very old; and Abishag the Shunammite ministered unto the king.

16. And Bath-sheba bowed, and did obeisance unto the king. And the king said, What wouldest thou?

What a pitiful sight David must have been, with the beautiful Abishag "ministering unto the King", as Bath-sheba entered his presence. Bath-sheba observed that the King was very old.

"And the damsel was very fair, and cherished the King, and ministered to him: but the King knew her not."

What a fitting epitaph is this for the gentleman whose acts we have just reviewed.

Chapter X.

The Rape of Tamar by Her Brother Amnon.

The love of brother and sister is one of the sweetest and most appealing of life's relationships. When this love is enhanced by the brother's chivalric attitude towards his sister, and he not only loves her tenderly, but seeks to act as her guardian and protector, we have a family relationship, the very embodiment of which "is a consummation devoutly to be wished."

When you see a brother anxious about the welfare of his sister, you can very confidently conclude that they are members of a family with the very highest ideals and principles. The love of brother and sister is one of those human ties which we remember with so much tenderness and mention with so much pride. Were this affection between brother and sister instilled in us in our childhood, there would be no need for fearful moments in later years regarding our children's development. Their characters will reflect their training. They will become not only an honor to their parents, but a credit to the community which is fortunate enough to have them as citizens. The finest impulses of life spring from this brotherly and sisterly devotion.

And how many men, remembering their sisters, are deterred from committing some misdeed towards another man's sister? And how many times have you heard a man say to another who boasts of his conquests, "Would you want that to happen to your sister?" Morality's cornerstone is shaped within the circle of the family. Learn the attitude of one towards the other and you have the key to that family's moral worth. Morality's most perfect instrument in measuring the calibre of a man is in determining his attitude towards the weaker sex. To instill this cherished relationship into the minds of our children should be our deep concern.

If it is by example and illustration that moral lessons are best inculcated; then it naturally follows that the books we instruct our children to read should contain stories which impress such examples upon their mind.

There are in circulation many books with such stories and examples, but the ministers of the church do not seem to be particularly interested in them. They are over-officious in their demand that the Bible be read in our public schools and its examples be impressed upon the minds of our children. So, as a means of enlightenment, we will relate the next story which follows in the Bible so that you may judge for yourself its value in uplifting morally the character of our people. It is needless to mention that your sensibilities will be shocked by what is to follow, unless the previous chapters of the Bible have revealed a sufficient amount of appalling stories to make you callous to anything that might still be related.

Remember, the story to follow comes from a book sanctified as the Holy Scriptures, and I wonder how many can read it without a feeling of repulsion and contempt for the book from which it is taken? How many will understand the mockery of such a name as "Holy Scriptures" upon the covers of the Bible? For its full significance, I quote the story without interruption.

Samuel 2, Chapter 13, Verses 1-14.

And it came to pass after this, that Absalom the son of David had a fair sister, whose name was Tamar; and Amnon the son of David loved her.

2. And Amnon was so vexed, that he fell sick for his sister Tamar; for she was a virgin; and Amnon thought it hard for him to do any thing to her.

3. But Amnon had a friend, whose name was Jonadab, the son of Shimeah David's brother: and Jonadab was a very subtle man.

4. And he said unto him, Why art thou, being the king's son, lean from day to day? wilt thou not tell me? And Amnon said unto him, I love Tamar my brother Absalom's sister.

5. And Jonadab said unto him, Lay thee down on thy bed, and make thyself sick: and when thy father cometh to see thee, say unto him, I pray thee, let my sister Tamar come, and give me meat, and dress the meat in my sight, that I may see it, and eat it at her hand.

6. So Amnon lay down, and made himself sick: and when the king was come to see him, Amnon said unto the king, I pray thee, let Tamar my sister come, and make me a couple of cakes in my sight, that I may eat at her hand.

7. Then David sent home to Tamar, saying, Go now to thy brother Amnon's house, and dress him meat.

8. So Tamar went to her brother Amnon's house; and he was laid down. And she took flour, and kneaded it, and made cakes in his sight, and did bake the cakes.

9. And she took a pan, and poured them out before him; but he refused to eat. And Amnon said, Have out all men from me. And they went out every man from him.

10. And Amnon said unto Tamar, Bring the meat into the chamber, that I may eat of thine hand. And Tamar took the cakes which she had made, and brought them into the chamber to Amnon her brother.

11. And when she had brought them unto him to eat, he took hold of her and said unto her, Come lie with me, my sister.

12. And she answered him, Nay, my brother, do not force me; for no such thing ought to be done in Israel: do not thou this folly.

13. And I, whither shall I cause my shame to go? and as for thee, thou shalt be as one of the fools in Israel. Now therefore, I pray thee, speak unto the king; for he will not withhold me from thee.

14. Howbeit he would not hearken unto her voice: but, being stronger than she, forced her, and lay with her.

The pleadings of his fair sister were of no avail. "Nay, my brother, do not force me," she cried; but, evidently bearing in mind the example set by his father David, Amnon, "being stronger than she, forced her, and lay with her."

Wouldn't this story be ten thousand times better if it depicted an altogether different scene -- a scene where a brother seeks, even to the sacrificing of his life, the protection of his sister?

So much for this foul deed. Amnon is well suited to be associated with the other Biblical men, and is truly a worthy son of his infamous father. His so-called "love" for his sister was not real love, but a brutal and lustful desire.

Samuel 2, Chapter 13, Verses 15-16.

15. Then Amnon hated her exceedingly; so that the hatred wherewith he hated her was greater than the love wherewith he had loved her. And Amnon said unto her, Arise, be gone.

16. He could not have treated the commonest woman with more brutality than he did his own sister, whom he should have protected against harm at all costs.

Samuel 2, Chapter 13, Verses 18-19.

18. And she had a garment of divers colours upon her: for with such robes were the king's daughters that were virgins apparelled. Then his servant brought her out, and bolted the door after her.

19. And Tamar put ashes on her head, and rent her garment of divers colours that was on her, and laid her hand on her head, and went on crying.

What happens to poor Tamar the story does not tell at this particular time.

Samuel 2, Chapter 13, Verse 20.

20. And Absalom her brother said unto her, Hath Amnon thy brother been with thee? but hold now thy peace, my sister: he is thy brother; regard not this thing. So Tamar remained desolate in her brother Absalom's house.

The story continues, and Absalom, after a period of two years, finally avenges the rape of his sister, by murdering Amnon.

Just think, this story of rape and incest, is quoted from the book that our children are taught to read in Sunday Schools; the book they are taught to hold in deep reverence, and respect above everything else in life; a book that they are forced to kiss if it happens to fall to the floor -- the kiss implying the love and holiness with which they regard it -- a book which has made mental slaves of them, and which must be worshipped with an undivided devotion. Even to question the authority of this book is the sacrilege of sacrilege.

Oh! the horror of it! It seems unbelievable that such a story, where a brother cunningly entices his sister into his room, under the pretext of being ill, and while she is engaged in preparing his food, orders all attendants to leave, and then ravishes her, could be found anywhere within the reach of children; and yet ignorant parents and stupid preachers, even to the extent of punishment, force the reading of this book upon children!!

Before passing on to the next story, let me ask this question: Is the Bible the book to which we should look for that sublime example of family relationship we all should try to emulate?

Answer that question in the sincerity of your own mind?

Chapter XI.

The Story of Ruth.

"It's love that makes the world go 'round," and those stories which depict love in its best and holiest sense, are ever dear to the heart of man. Surely it would appear certain that the sweetest story of love would be found in the book represented as being of "divine inspiration" and containing the highest sentiments of love. You would expect it to detail love in its most cherished and hallowed way and to be ever a guide and inspiration for the children of the earth to follow.

Whenever we speak of love -- that precious bond between man and woman -- we quite naturally think of the immortal production, "Romeo and Juliet." But it may be enlightening to some to learn that "Romeo and Juliet" is not to be found in the Bible. This wonderful classic of love's emotion is the product of a human being by the name of William Shakespeare. We might well boast of the Bible and its value were it to contain this precious document of love.

But the love story of the Bible is found in The Book of Ruth, and let us hope it contains the philosophy, the inspiration, the humanity and the love of one for the other, found in that love story of Shakespeare.

It is by example and inspiration, more than by any other means, that we advance intellectually and morally. It is example which inspires us to emulate the great forward steps that have been made in the ethical and moral life of the human race. For that reason examples are of the utmost importance in elevating the moral life of man.

It is "setting the good example" to the child, which prompts him, above everything else, to develop moral character. How often is it the bad example that is responsible for the warping of the child's moral fibre? If it is the example that is so influential in determining the moral development of our children, it therefore becomes our solemn duty to see that only the best of examples are put before our children for their guidance.

It is our duty as parents, if we are concerned at all with the happiness of our children and the welfare of our community, to see that the pernicious and the degrading influences are avoided and those tender emotions that make for love, and honor, and integrity are implanted into the very depths of their hearts. The Bible contains "love stories"; but these stories are such that I do not think you would consider them the ideal ones that your daughter should follow.

Were your daughter to follow the action of Ruth in the attainment of what she desired, what would be your opinion of her? And if you object to the behavior of Ruth, what right have you to insist that your child read the Bible for inspiration and example? And if the Bible's narrative is such that it deserves your condemnation, of what spineless material are you made that you are not prompted to protest against the dissemination of the Bible's immoralities and degrading influences? If the Bible admonished our young women to avoid the actions of Ruth in the attainment of what she desired, then we could, with pride, point to its moral. But it does nothing of the kind. It is just another one of the Bible's samples of prostitution and sexual debauchery.

Although the entire Book of Ruth is quite short, I do not think it necessary to quote it in its entirety. The story relates how a famine covered the land and how a man and his wife and two sons journeyed to another country to escape starvation; while there, the two sons married two daughters of that land. In a short time all the male members of the family died, leaving the mother and her two daughters-in-law without male companionship and support. And from here we begin our story.

I quote The Book of Ruth, Chapter 1, Verses 1-13.

Now it came to pass in the days when the judges ruled, that there was a famine in the land. And a certain man of Beth-lehem-judah went to sojourn in the country of Moab, he, and his wife, and his two sons.

2. And the name of the man was Elimelech, and the name of his wife Naomi, and the name of his two sons Mahlon and Chilion, Ephrathites of Beth-lehem-judah. And they came into the country of Moab, and continued there.

3. And Elimelech Naomi's husband died; and she was left, and her two sons.

4. And they took them wives of the women of Moab; the name of the one was Orpah, and the name of the other Ruth: and they dwelt there about ten years.

5. And Mahlon and Chilion died also both of them; and the woman was left of her two sons and her husband.

6. Then she arose with her daughters in law, that she might return from the country of Moab: for she had heard in the country of Moab how that the Lord had visited his people in giving them bread.

7. Wherefore she went forth out of the place where she was, and her two daughters in law with her; and they went on the way to return unto the land of Judah.

8. And Naomi said unto her two daughters in law, Go, return each to her mother's house: the Lord deal kindly with you, as ye have dealt with the dead, and with me.

9 The Lord grant you that ye may find rest, each of you in the house of her husband. Then she kissed them; and they lifted up their voice, and wept.

10. And they said unto her, Surely we will return with thee unto thy people.

11. And Naomi said, Turn again, my daughters: why will ye go with me? are there yet any more sons in my womb, that they may be your husbands?

12. Turn again, my daughters, go your way; for I am too old to have a husband. If I should say, I have hope, if I should have a husband also to night, and should also bear sons;

13. Would ye tarry for them till they were grown? would ye stay for them from having husbands? nay, my daughters: for it grieveth me much for your sakes that the hand of the Lord is gone out against me.

It was certainly nice for the two daughters-in-law to cling to their mother-in-law in this crisis, but let me repeat, as an edifying thought, the words of the mother when she says, "Turn again my daughters, why will you go with me? Are there yet any more sons in my womb, that they may be your husbands?" This is not the only edifying thought expressed in the narrative and we quote again, "Turn again, my daughters, go your way; for I am too old to have a husband. If I should say, I have hope, if I should have a husband also to-night, and should also bear sons." I am inclined to think that if there were any men around Orpah and Ruth would have wanted them, since marriage was what Naomi so anxiously desired for them. How foolish it would have been for them to wait for the birth and growth of Naomi's child, "if she should have a husband also to-night, and should also bear sons"?

Aside from_ what the narrative implies and aside from the delicacy with which it is expressed, no one can gainsay that the above quotations do not make for a sensible sex education for our young.

The Book of Ruth, Chapter 1, Verses 14-19.

14. And they lifted up their voice, and wept again: and Orpah kissed her mother in law; but Ruth clave unto her.

15. And she said, Behold, thy sister in law is gone back unto her people, and unto her gods: return thou after thy sister in law.

16. And Ruth said, Entreat me not to leave thee, or to return from following after thee: for whither thou goest, I will go; and where thou lodgest, I will lodge: thy people shall be my people, and thy God my God.

17. Where thou diest, will I die, and there will I be buried: the Lord do so to me, and more also, if aught but death part thee and me.

18. When she saw that she was steadfastly minded to go with her, then she left speaking unto her.

19. So they two went until they came to Beth-lehem. And it came to pass, when they were come to Beth-lehem, that all the city was moved about them, and they said, Is this Naomi?

Because of Ruth's loyalty, Naomi, her mother-in-law, was constantly on the look-out for her welfare and particularly anxious to secure a husband for her. It is Naomi's actions in this matter which bring us to the heart of the story. It is what she makes Ruth do that so concerns us.

The Book of Ruth, Chapter 3, Verses 1-4.

Then Naomi her mother in law said unto her, My daughter, shall I not seek rest for thee, that it may be well with thee?

2. And now is not Boaz of our kindred, with whose maidens thou wast? Behold, he winnoweth barley to night in the threshingfloor.

3. Wash thyself therefore, and anoint thee, and put thy raiment upon thee, and get thee down to the floor: but make not thyself known unto the man, until he shall have done eating and drinking.

4. And it shall be, when he lieth down. that thou shalt mark the place where he shall lie, and thou shalt go in, and uncover his feet, and lay thee down; and he will tell thee what thou shalt do.

This is certainly a pleasing situation. "And it shall be, when he lieth down, that thou shalt mark the place where he shall lie, and thou shalt go in, and uncover his feet, and lay thee down; and he will tell thee what to do." "He will tell thee what to do" is just enough, were our taste for the lascivious, to arouse our curiosity for more details. Ruth was well aware what was to take place, as she assented to the instructions in the verse following.

The Book of Ruth, Chapter 3, Verses 5-6.

5. And she said unto her, All that thou sayest unto me I will do.

6. And she went down unto the floor, and did according to all that her mother in law bade her.

That Ruth followed the instructions of her mother-in-law to the letter, is revealed in the next verse, and we inquisitively await her action especially since we are told that when she "uncover his feet, and lay thee down, he will tell thee what to do."

The Book of Ruth, Chapter 3, Verse 7.

7. And when Boaz had eaten and drunk, and his heart was merry, he went to lie down at the end of the heap of corn: and she came softly, and uncovered his feet, and laid her down.

What a situation! After eating and drinking to your heart's content, to lie down for a sweet slumber and have a delightful and willing young lady to uncover your feet, lie down next to you, and be your bed-fellow until --

The Book of Ruth, Chapter 3, Verse 8.

8. And it came to pass at midnight, that the man was afraid, and turned himself: and, behold, a woman lay at his feet.

Now put yourself in Boaz's position for a moment, and would you not have been "afraid" to find in the very dead of night, a lovely young lady lying next to you, wholly unannounced and unexpected?

The Book of Ruth, Chapter 3, Verse 9.

9. And he said, Who art thou? And she answered, I am Ruth thine handmaid spread therefore thy skirt over thine handmaid: for thou art a near kinsman.

"Who art thou?" Boaz nervously, but very rightly, asks. And it is very fortunate he had that much presence of mind, and Ruth answered coyly and with all the appeal of the feminine instinct, "I am Ruth, thy handmaid: therefore spread thy skirt over thy handmaid," which was certainly an encouraging sign on her part. They wore loose apparel in those days and when she said to Boaz, "spread thy skirt over thy handmaid," there was much significance attached to that suggestion.

The Book of Ruth, Chapter 3, Verses 10-11.

10. And he said, Blessed be thou of the Lord, my daughter: for thou hast shewed more kindness in the latter end than at the beginning, inasmuch as thou followedst not young men, whether poor or rich.

11. And now, my daughter, fear not; I will do to thee all that thou requirest: for all the city of my people doth know that thou art a virtuous woman.

No wonder Boaz blessed the Lord for her, and did unto her all that she requirest. But I doubt very much whether all the people considered her a virtuous woman after this little lark. People are rather suspicious of young girls who spend the night with a man.

I wonder what Boaz meant when he said, "for thou hast shown more kindness in the latter end than at the beginning?" Could it have been that Ruth at first repulsed his attentions and later willingly submitted to him?

The Book of Ruth, Chapter 3, Verses 12-13.

12. And now it is true that I am thy near kinsman: howbeit there is a kinsman nearer than I.

13. Tarry this night, and it shall be in the morning, that if he will perform unto thee the part of a kinsman, well; let him do the kinsman's part: but if he will not do the part of a kinsman to thee, then will I do the part of a kinsman to thee, as the Lord liveth: lie down until the morning.

If you think Boaz meant anything but the purest of Platonic relationship when he told Ruth at midnight, mind you, to "lie down until the morning," and that, as the Lord liveth, he would do the kinsman part to her, you are assured of this truth from the following.

The Book of Ruth, Chapter 3, Verse 14.

14. And she lay at his feet until the morning: and she rose up before one could know another. And he said, Let it not be known that a woman came into the floor.

There is somewhat of a slight contradiction in the verse above. Certainly if it were midnight when Boaz discovered Ruth, and she lay there with him until morning, there was plenty of time for one to "know another." The translators, evidently realizing the suggestion contained in this verse, inserted the phrase, "she rose up before one could know another," to circumvent the thought that would naturally arise at such a situation. The situation and inference, however, are only too plain. His very significant remark, "Let it not be known that a woman came into the floor," needs no comment.

The Book of Ruth, Chapter 3, Verses 15-16.

15. Also he said, Bring the vail that thou hast upon thee, and hold it. And when she held it, he measured six measures of barley, and laid it on her: and she went into the city.

16. And when she came to her mother in law, she said, Who art thou, my daughter? And she told her all that the man had done to her.

Enough has been quoted from this narrative to classify it as being too suggestive for cultural reading, especially to growing youth. "And she told her all that the man had done to her," is sufficient unto itself to brand it with the mark of the lascivious. That Ruth was fully compensated for "all that the man had done to her," is amplified in the following.

The Book of Ruth, Chapter 3, Verses 17-18.

17. And she said, These six measures of barley gave he me; for he said to me, Go not empty unto thy mother in law.

18. Then said she, Sit still, my daughter, until thou know how the matter will fall: for the man will not be in rest, until he have finished the thing this day.

What Naomi meant when she told Ruth to "sit still, my daughter, until thou know how the matter will fall," admits of your own interpretation and I will not give mine. Of one thing I am sure, and that is this: If your daughter, or any man's daughter chose Ruth's method of securing a husband, what would be your thoughts about the matter? Would you consider it elevating? Would you consider it respectable? Would you sanction it as being the proper course of courtship? Or would you more properly condemn it as being abhorrent to our moral sensibilities? If you read this story in any other book than the Bible, would you not condemn it as being suggestive and vulgar? Haven't stories with less "color" than this one been judged obscene? If we are to look to the Bible for our source of knowledge and our guidance through life, is this story of Ruth conducive to such an end?

Now, honor bright, let us be fair and honest with each other. Wouldn't it have made a glorious difference; wouldn't an immeasurable benefit have resulted, had the story of Ruth imparted to the marriageable girl or prospective bride the essential knowledge so vital to her welfare and happiness in the marital state? Knowledge of the proper sex relation; knowledge of maternal care; yes, knowledge of Birth Control; not instead to suggest that she lay on the floor, next to a man all night as an advertisement for her charms and physical credentials of her marriageability?

And to cap the climax, marriage ceremonies are solemnized by the bride and groom, placing their hands, in the holy bonds of matrimony, upon the covers of the Bible, as a benediction of God to their sacred union!

Chapter XII.

King Solomon and His Songs.

Before quoting the erotic utterances from the Songs of Solomon, it may be permissible to make mention of an incident in the life of Solomon which possesses a rather unique angle and which gives an interesting index to his conduct. You remember when Abishag, the young and beautiful virgin, was ministering to David to give him "heat" that he might "know her," Bath-sheba, his wife, approached him, and in pleading tones, begged David, that Solomon, her child, might inherit the throne of Israel. She made this plea because word had just been brought to her by Nathan, the prophet, that another and elder son, Adonijah, by another wife, had set up a throne and proclaimed himself King of Israel. David granted her request, if you remember. and upon his death, Solomon ascended the throne of Israel.

Being denied the right to the cherished kingship, Adonijah wanted the next best thing that David possessed, and we begin our narrative by quoting Kings 1, Chapter 2, Verses 12-14.

12. Then sat Solomon upon the throne of David his father; and his kingdom was established greatly.

13. And Adonijah the son of Haggith came to Bath-sheba the mother of Solomon. And she said, Comest thou peaceably? And he said, Peaceably.

14. He said moreover, I have somewhat to say unto thee. And she said, Say on.

Adonijah has evidently buried his disappointment at not being able to reign over Israel and shows his manhood by coming to Bath-sheba and proclaiming peace. This is a very encouraging sign, for, several thousand were generally killed when such a situation arose among these blood-thirsty savages. "Comest thou peaceably?" asks Bath-sheba, and Adonijah replies, "Peaceably." But -- and this forms the basis of a significant incident -- "I have somewhat to say unto thee," and Bath-sheba, with all the refinement and dignity of a King's mother, answers, "Say on."

Kings 1, Chapter 2, Verses 15-17.

15. And he said, Thou knowest that the kingdom was mine, and that all Israel set their faces on me, that I should reign: howbeit the kingdom is turned about, and is become my brother's: for it was his from the Lord.

16. And now I ask one petition of thee, deny me not. And she said unto him, Say on.

17. And he said, Speak, I pray thee, unto Solomon the king, (for he will not say thee nay,) that he give me Abishag the Shunammite to wife.

After all, it was a very small price to ask in exchange for the giving up of a kingdom; a kingdom with sufficient power to secure for yourself any woman that you desired. But aside from that, is not the situation one of high spiritual value? Is it not conducive to moral elevation to ask as your wife a young lady who but recently had lain in the bosom of your father for the purpose of giving him "heat"? As for Abishag, she no doubt was anxious, after the heroic endeavor to have David "know her," to secure as a husband a younger and more virile man. Bath-sheba sees the justice of Adonijah's petition, and possibly remembering with a bit of jealousy the scene of David and Abishag agrees to speak to Solomon in behalf of Adonijah in his quest for the beautiful virgin. As Solomon's reign is noted for its wisdom, let us note carefully with what wisdom he executes his first official act.

Kings 1, Chapter 2, Verses 18-20.

18. And Bath-sheba said, Well; I will speak for thee unto the king.

19. Bath-sheba therefore went unto king Solomon, to speak unto him for Adonijah. And the king rose up to meet her, and bowed himself unto her, and sat down on his throne, and caused a seat to be set for the king's mother; and she sat on his right hand.

20. Then she said, I desire one small petition of thee; I pray thee, say me not nay. And the king said unto her, Ask on, my mother; for I will not say thee nay.

After all, it was a very small matter, when we take into consideration that Solomon was to possess seven hundred wives and three hundred concubines. And then there is another thought to be taken into consideration. What would Solomon do with Abishag? Would this wise man (wisest who ever lived according to the Jews) want her for himself after she had lain in his father's bosom? Or was the beauty of Abishag so captivating that it overshadowed this objection?

For the answer to Bath-sheba's request of Adonijah's desire, we must continue with the Biblical narrative; but remember Solomon's assurance to his mother when she asks for the granting of this "one small petition," he answers, "I will not say thee nay."

Kings 1, Chapter 2, Verses 21-22.

21. And she said, Let Abishag the Shunammite be given to Adonijah thy brother to wife.

22. And king Solomon answered and said unto his mother, And why dost thou ask Abishag the Shunammite for Adonijah? ask for him the kingdom also; for he is mine elder brother; even for him, and for Abiathar the priest, and for Joab the son of Zeruiah.

What! did Solomon consider the beauty of this Shunammite maid equal to the possession of his kingdom? "Why, Mother dear, why don't you ask me for the entire kingdom"? whispered Solomon with a slight curl upon his lips. Solomon not only inherited his father's kingdom, but also had a desire to possess this beautiful virgin. For Adonijah's insolence for even making such a request, read the judgment this "wise" man of Israel inflicts upon him.

Kings 1, Chapter 2, Verses 23-25.

23. Then king Solomon sware by the Lord, saying, God do so to me and more also, if Adonijah have not spoken this word against his own life.

24. Now therefore, as the Lord liveth, which hath established me, and set me on the throne of David my father, and who hath made me a house, as he promised, Adonijah shall be put to death this day.

25. And King Solomon sent by the hand of Benaiah the son of Jehoiada; and he fell upon him that he died.

So much for this little episode. It is indeed a very difficult thing to make continual comment upon the atrocities of these Biblical characters, and so I will let the matter rest with your judgment. My only comment is this: Perhaps while in the caress of this beautiful young woman, Solomon was inspired to write the lovely songs from which I will quote a few extracts. The Bible from which the following verses are taken, has as a caption at the beginning of the chapter:

"The Church and Christ Congratulate One Another."

If the "Church" is a woman and "Christ" a man, well might they.

I quote The Songs of Solomon, Chapter 1, Verse 13.

13. A bundle of myrrh is my well beloved unto me; he shall lie all night betwixt my breasts.

I must again confess my lack of spiritual understanding to imagine that this verse represents a "loving" meeting between the Son of God and his church on earth.

It is my opinion, and there is abundant evidence to prove it true, that the early fathers of the church, realizing the eroticism of the Songs of

Solomon, falsely captioned the verses to detract from their passionate suggestions. For what hypocrisy it is to say that these songs represent Christ and his church, when they were written long before Christ was born and before the Christian church came into existence. It is pure hypocrisy to so caption these passionate love songs.

The Songs of Solomon, Chapter 3, Verses 1-2. The caption above this song is: "The Church's Fight and Victory In Temptation."

What is your opinion of it?

By night on my bed, I sought him whom my soul loveth: I sought him, but I found him not.

2. I will rise now, and go about the city in the streets, and in the broad ways I will seek him whom my soul loveth: I sought him, but I found him not.

For wonderful prophetic knowledge we must bow in reverence to the Bible. Who would dream that, after 2,000 years, this verse would be just as applicable as it was when first written? Were the "broad ways" of Biblical times the same as our own Broadway?

The Songs of Solomon, Chapter 3, Verses 3-4.

3. The watchmen that go about the city found me: *to whom I said, Saw ye him whom my soul loveth?*

4. It was but a little that I passed from them, but I found him whom my soul loveth: I held him, and would not let him go, until I had brought him into my mother's house, and into the chamber of her that conceived me.

Remember that at the beginning of this song I quoted the caption which appears in the Bible, that this song was "The Church's Fight and Victory in Temptation," and can you tell me how any sane person can interpret the following words to mean what this caption is supposed to infer? "I found him whom my soul loveth; I held him, and would not let him go, until I brought him into my mothers house, and into the chamber of her that conceived me." If the "church" was fighting temptation, I am of the conviction that in this instance, she yielded to it. What do you think of such a "victory"?

The next song of Solomon's is captioned

"Christ Setteth Forth the Graces of the Church."

And I want you to read carefully what follows in order to note how perfectly and minutely the description fits the title.

The Songs of Solomon, Chapter 4, Verses 1-2.

Behold, thou art fair, my love; behold, thou art fair; thou hast doves' eyes within thy locks: thy hair is as a flock of goats, that appear from mount Gilead.

2. Thy teeth are like a flock of sheep that are even shorn, which came up from the washing; whereof every one bear twins, and none is barren among them.

If you have never seen the "teeth" of the church you can very easily get a glimpse of them by reading "The Conflict of Science and Religion" by Professor John W. Draper.

The Songs of Solomon, Chapter 4, Verses 3-5.

3. Thy lips are like a thread of scarlet, and thy speech is comely: thy temples are like a piece of a pomegranate within thy locks.

4. Thy neck is like the tower of David builded for an armoury, whereon there hang a thousand bucklers, all shields of mighty men.

5. Thy two breasts are like two young roes that are twins, which feed among the lilies.

Did you ever see anything on a church or a part of a church that looked like the breasts of a woman? You haven't, neither have I; nor does this description refer to a building. This song gives such a perfect "outline" and "form" of a "church" that I will quote it entire.

The Songs of Solomon, Chapter 4, Verses 6-9.

6. Until the day break, and the shadows flee away, I will get me to the mountain of myrrh, and to the hill of frankincense.

7. Thou art all fair, my love, there is no spot in thee.

8. Come with me from Lebanon, my spouse, with me from Lebanon: look from the top of Amana, from the top of Shenir and Hermon, from the lions' dens, from the mountains of the leopards.

9 Thou hast ravished my heart, my sister, my spouse; thou hast ravished my heart with one of thine eyes, with one chain of thy neck.

Let me repeat the expression, I am sure we have all heard, but never in reference to a building. "Thou hast ravished my heart, my sister; thou hast ravished my heart with one of thine eyes, with one chain of thy neck."

The Songs of Solomon, Chapter 4, Verse 10.

10. How fair is thy love, my sister, my spouse! how much better is thy love than wine! and the smell of thine ointments than all spices!

We have also heard that before and it was never uttered to a church.

The Songs of Solomon, Chapter 4, Verses 11-12.

11. Thy lips, O my spouse, drop as the honeycomb: honey and milk are under thy tongue; and the smell of thy garments is like the smell of Lebanon.

12. A garden inclosed is my sister, my spouse; a spring shut up, a fountain sealed.

Certainly the church was never deserving of such a tribute. And now to conclude this choice erotic song.

The Songs of Solomon, Chapter 4, Verses 13-16.

13. Thy plants are an orchard of pomegranates, with pleasant fruits; camphire, with spikenard,

14. Spikenard and saffron; calamus and cinnamon, with all trees of frankincense; myrrh and aloes, with all the chief spices:

15. A fountain of gardens, a well of living waters, and streams from Lebanon.

16. Awake. O north wind; and come, thou south; blow upon my garden, that the spices thereof may flow out. Let my beloved come into his garden, and eat his pleasant fruits.

If in this song "Christ Setteth Forth the Graces of the Church" I would like to hear what he has to say about the graces of the female form.

Mothers usually sing their children to sleep with a sweet lullaby. To those devoutly religious mothers, who hold the Bible so tenderly and preciously, and revere it as the inspired word of God, and who are so anxious to have their children acquainted with the Bible and receive religious instruction, I question if even they would sing the following delicate verses from the Songs of Solomon, which are found in Chapter 5, and are captioned,

"The Church Having a Taste of Christ's Love is Sick of Love."

Can you imagine the audacity of the church itself saying it is "sick of Christ's love"?

The Songs of Solomon, Chapter 5, Verse 1.

I am come into my garden, my sister, my spouse: I have gathered my myrrh with my spice; I have eaten my honeycomb with my honey; I have drunk my wine with my milk: eat, O friends; drink, yea, drink abundantly, O beloved.

Eating and drinking abundantly have always been associated with the lustful and have never to my knowledge been symbolical of the church. Praying and fasting have been church functions. But to continue, and reveal the reason why the church became sick of Christ's love.

The Songs of Solomon, Chapter 5, Verses 2-4.

2. I sleep, but my heart waketh: it is the voice of my beloved that knocketh, saying, Open to me, my sister, my love, my dove, my undefiled: for my head is filled with dew, and my locks with the drops of the night.

3. I have put off my coat; how shall I put it on? I have washed my feet; how shall I defile them?

4. My beloved put in his hand by the hole of the door, -.

Take your Bible in hand and finish this song for yourself. If you are particularly keen for literature of this kind, note well these verses taken at random.

The Songs of Solomon, Chapter 7, Verses 1-3.

By the way these are a "further description of the Church's graces."

How beautiful are thy feet with shoes, O prince's daughter! the joints of thy thighs are like jewels, the work of the hands of a cunning workman.

2. Thy navel is like a round goblet, which wanteth not liquor: thy belly is like a heap of wheat set about with lilies.

3. Thy two breasts are like two young roes that are twins.

Evidently the songster was greatly enthused over the woman's breasts, for he again says:

The Songs of Solomon, Chapter 7, Verses 7-8.

7. This thy stature is like to a palm tree, and thy breasts to clusters of grapes.

8. I said, I will go up to the palm tree, I will take hold of the boughs thereof: now also thy breasts shall be as clusters of the vine, and the smell of thy nose like apples.

One final quotation from the last chapter of Solomon's Songs and we will pass on to the next of the Bible's narratives.

The Songs of Solomon, Chapter 8, Verse 8, suggests this question:

8. We have a little sister, and she hath no breasts: what shall we do for our sister in the day when she shall be spoken for?

The Songs of Solomon, Chapter 8, Verse 14.

14. Make haste, my beloved, and be thou like to a roe or to a young hart upon the mountains of spices.

The above verse is interpreted by the learned Christians as being "The Church prayeth for Christ's coming," and this in spite of the fact, in a few verses back, she was sick of his love.

Only recently I heard a professor of literature in one of our largest universities say that the Songs of Solomon were valuable pieces of erotic poetry, but should never be in a volume within the reach of a child. He said they should be read only by mature minds in appreciation of their style of expression.[8]

I do not wish to go into a lengthy discussion of these erotic songs, but I do wish to mention the fact that the English translation of them has been greatly modified. It is stated upon the most reliable authority that, in the original language, the Songs of Solomon are absolutely unmentionable. To classify these songs as being the love of Christ for his Church is one of the boldest pieces of insolence and mendacity in the hypocritical career of the Church.

Are the people so credulous as to believe that these erotic utterances were inspired by God?

---

[8] Prof. Randolph Sommerville, N. Y. University -- Dept. of Literature -- in address delivered from radio station WJZ, January 6, 1925.

Chapter XIII.

The Book of Esther.

I had every intention of dissecting this story in the same manner as I have revealed the other items in the Bible, but the lewd suggestions and immoralities of this story are only a side issue to its main import. Compared with the stories already related, the story of Esther is a mildly sugar-coated narrative. But it contains a scene and a method of which no reader of the Bible should be ignorant and I will for the sake of exposure make mention of it.

It deals with a King who demands that his queenly wife enter the chambers of his drunken revelry, presumably wearing only her crown, to display her beautiful body before the eyes of his bawdy guests, for the Bible very plainly says, "she was very fair to look upon." When Queen Vashti refused to obey the command of King Ahasuerus to degrade herself, and was dismissed because she upheld her womanly honor, it took the King nearly three years, by his personally tested method, to find a woman to replace her in the Royal household. The details of King Ahasuerus's method of replacing the Queen beggars my prosaic pen, so I will let the Bible describe it for you.

I quote The Book of Esther, Chapter 2, Verses 12-13.

12. Now when every maid's turn was come to go in to king Ahasuerus, after that she had been twelve months, according to the manner of the women, (for so were the days of their purifications accomplished, to wit, six months with oil of myrrh, and six months with sweet odours, and with other things for the purifying of the women,)

13. Then thus came every maiden unto the king; whatsoever she desired was given her to go with her out of the house of the women unto the king's house.

Mind you, for twelve months these maidens were being prepared in the Royal Beauty Parlor to favor the King. For six months they were anointed with oil of myrrh and for six months with "other sweet odours." Each and every one, after such treatment, must have presented a "dish" truly "fit to set before a King." This most "luscious" dish was "served" each evening to the King's taste.

The Book of Esther, Chapter 2, Verse 14.

14. In the evening she went, and on the morrow she returned into the second house of the women, to the custody of Shaashgaz, the king's chamberlain, which kept the concubines: she came in unto the king no more, except the king delighted in her, and that she were called by name.

"In the evening she went in and on the morrow she returned," is sufficient unto itself. Your imagination is not required for further elucidation. You are not asked to visualize what took place each night in the King's palace. "She came in unto the King no more, except the King delighted in her, and that she was called by name." This merely means that some of the girls were so captivating the King required a "second testing" in order to determine their acceptability. The closeness of the contest must have been thrilling to all concerned.

This testing method employed by King Ahasuerus by which a virgin entered his chambers in the evening and went not out until the morning, in order that he might select the most desirable one, consumed a period of nearly three years, and if the performance continued night after night, which no doubt it did, and the Bible leads one to believe it did, more than 1,000 girls were sacrificed upon the altar of lust.

But now for the triumph of the Jewess Esther.

The Book of Esther, Chapter 2, Verses 15-17.

15. Now when the turn of Esther, the daughter of Abihail the uncle of Mordecai, who had taken her for his daughter, was come to go in unto the king, she required nothing but what Hegai the king's chamberlain, the keeper of the women, appointed. And Esther obtained favour in the sight of all them that looked upon her.

16. So Esther was taken unto king Ahasuerus into his house royal in the tenth month, which is the month Tebeth, in the seventh year of his reign.

17. And the king loved Esther above all the women, and she obtained grace and favour in his sight more than all the virgins; so that he set the royal crown upon her head, and made her queen instead of Vashti.

But before passing this story let me express this thought. This story of Esther once again reveals the complete reversal of what the Bible is supposed to teach. Instead of Queen Vashti being pictured as the Ideal of Womanhood, Esther, who prostituted herself, is set forth as the pattern and example for the world. Instead of the narration disclosing the true qualities that a woman should possess as Queen, the Bible details the most revolting method whereby a woman is selected for her lustful attractiveness. Not intelligence, companionability, sympathetic understanding, womanliness and love, but the choice bedfellow that she would make is the successful qualification for acceptance as wife and queen.

As I stated before, the real intent of this story does not belong technically within the scope of my subject, but the immoral performance of making more than 1,000 young girls submit to the embrace of a man that he may select the most satisfying one was too degrading an act not to call to your attention in unmasking the Bible.

The story itself, with its hideous vindictiveness, you are urged to read entire. Then you will be able to grasp more fully the real import of the story.

I now come to the end of the Old Testament and were I to insert as part of this book all the filthy sayings and lewd suggestions of this part of the Bible I fear I would never finish my task until I had copied almost word for word all that the Old Testament contains. But if what it contains, as already quoted in the preceding pages of this book, is convincing to you that the Old Testament is a benefit to civilization, then you are in perfect accord with William Jennings Bryan's statement "that the Jews have given to the Christian world its greatest heritage."

And yet, peculiar as it may seem, in exchange for this priceless heritage, the Christians have "given" to the Jews a series of persecutions unequaled in the annals of human warfare. This I suppose is the quality of the Brotherhood of Man that naturally manifests itself after a complete conversion to the Bible's precepts. History proves this contention to be true; do not the different Christian sects "love" one another to the point of slaughter and extermination? Does not the church itself grow "sick of love" according to the Bible annotators?

If you do not agree with William Jennings Bryan about what he believed the Bible has done for the human race, then possibly you are in accord with me when I maintain that the Old Testament is one of the most immoral books in circulation.

Chapter XIV.

The New Testament.

The Old Testament is so-called because it is supposed to contain the first "Will" of God. And by the word "Will" is meant the same instrument that a person executes to dispose of his possessions after his death.

The believers in the Bible do not think God is dead, although a great many people feel sure that "he" does not exist. The Bible believers insist that God gave that book to the human race to be their guide in all earthly matters; and that it contains the sum-total of all there is to know; the infallible code of morals by which all should live their lives, and the secret for the preservation of their souls after death. For hundreds of years the "blood of the innocents" has been spilled to maintain this belief.

The New Testament is supposed to be the "last will and testament" of God. Just as a person may make a will and after a number of years decide to change some of his bequests, and executes another, so God, according to the Christian believer, elaborated upon his original covenant.

The Jews do not accept this "last will and testament" of God, and therefore reject it as being unworthy of consideration. The Jews believe the Messiah is yet to come, and that his appearance will be signalized by his riding upon the back of an ass.[9] Their attitude is very similar to the actions of people who refuse to accept the "last will and testament" of some of their relatives when it deprives them of bequests which were stipulated in a previous covenant.

It does seem a bit irregular that the Jews, being God's "Chosen People," should not welcome the issuance of a "second will"; and yet if God found another upon whom to place his affection, it is quite natural that his chosen people would reject this "New Testament" and maintain that it is not a true will; that it is fraudulent; that it was written under duress, and question the maker's mental capabilities at the time of its writing.

As the situation stands to-day, the difference of opinion regarding these two testaments of God has caused more sorrow, bloodshed, harm, devilment, misery and devastation than any other single item in the life and history of the human race. It would have been a thousand, thousand times better had God not made, as the legal phraseology terms it, this codicil. Like a dissatisfied heir, the human race might well

---

[9] Zechariah 9-9.

say to God: "If the Bible is the best you can give us, we don't want it. We would be better off without it."

Can you imagine the puerility of showing to a distinguished visitor from another planet, called here by some marvelous instrumentality like the radio, the Bible as our greatest legacy in life?

As we did not have to go very far into the pages of the Old Testament to encounter stories which shocked our moral sense, so early in the pages of the New Testament we find stories of an equally objectionable nature.

Before proceeding with a review of the birth of Christ as recorded in the New Testament, it might be said in justice to those who are so deluded as to actually believe that Christ was begotten in a miraculous way and is the "Son of God," the truth of the matter cannot be overlooked because of their convictions and feelings. A great many people believe a great many impossible things that must nevertheless be analyzed and publicly ridiculed in order to bring these people to their senses.

How true are the words of Mark Twain, when he says: "Power, money, persuasion, supplication, persecution -- these can lift at a colossal humbug -- push it a little -- weaken it a little, century after century; but only laughter can blow it to rags and atoms at a blast. Against the assault of laughter nothing can stand."[10]

I have often remarked, that if the Bible said that Moses stood on his eye-lid while God wrote the Ten Commandments with an in-growing toenail, the credulous would find no difficulty in believing it. And why should they? If it is a question of belief and faith what difference does its improbability make? I have read Mark Twain's "War Prayer" with all the solemnity of a preacher reading the Ten Commandments, to a number of devout Christians, and each and every one expressed the deepest feeling and admiration for it, and yet Mark Twain's "War Prayer" is as fine a bit of satire as there is in the English language, and well worthy of the pen of the great Voltaire. Mighty are the possibilities of faith!

It is truly a terrible thing, as Ingersoll says, to take away the consolation that naturally arises from a belief in eternal fire, but it is a holy joy to apply a little of this eternal fire to the body of a Bruno for his devilment in trying to rob the people of this great consolation.

When Columbus maintained that the earth was round, he was denounced and characterized as crazy, and when he set out on his memorable voyage to find a new way to India, and incidentally discovered the New World, the superstitious fell upon their knees and

---

[10] "Mysterious Stranger," page 142.

prayed their God to save him from the horrible destruction of falling into an eternal abyss. Was Columbus crazy or were the religious believers sufferers of insanity?

Galileo put a crude telescope to the sky and discovered our true relation to the universe, and proved the earth's rotation 'round the Sun. For his discovery of this great truth and his achievements in the scientific realm, what did these preservers of the faith and believers in the great consolation of eternal fire do to this great and grand benefactor of man? Let me quote the words of Professor John W. Draper:[11]

"He was declared to have brought upon himself the penalties of heresy. On his knees, with his hand on the Bible, he was compelled to adjure and curse the doctrine of the movement of the earth. What a spectacle. This venerable man, the most illustrious of his age, forced by the threat of death to deny facts which his judges as well as himself knew to be true! He was then committed to prison, treated with remorseless severity during the remaining ten years of his life, and was denied burial in consecrated ground. Must not that be false which requires for its support so much imposture, so much barbarity? The opinions thus defended by the Inquisition are now objects of derision of the whole civilized world."

Instances and examples could be given to fill an entire volume, where the progress of the world has been maintained only in the face of the most stubborn opposition from the religious believers who set up the cry that their faith is being destroyed. Even upon the invention of the airplane, some ministers denounced its success as being impious, as man had no right to enter into "God's domain"!

The Bible has been flaunted into the face of every forward and progressive step of the human race and had it continued successfully we would still be following the leadership of Abraham, Isaac and Jacob and living in constant fear of the damnation and hell fire of Jesus Christ. Slavery, polygamy, drudgery and ignorance would still be our lot, and the Dark Ages would be something that only the future could refer to.

A believer in Spiritualism finds its doctrines and fraudulent manifestations just as sacred as does a believer in the Divinity of Christ. The "consolation" arising from a belief in Spiritualism is not a deterrent to its exposure. Preying upon the tender feelings and ignorance of a person is a crime even if the delusion of the victim is complete. And as Spiritualism is unmercifully attacked and exposed because of its deception and falseness, so must the Divinity of Christ suffer the same fate because of its monumental humbuggery and fraud. The ignorant and the superstitious must give way to the intelligent. Fraud and falsehood, no matter how "sacred," must be replaced by fact and truth.

---

[11] "Conflict between Religion and Science," pages 170, 171.

As fraud in spiritualist manifestations is punishable by law, so should the deception of Christianity and its fraudulent promises be subject to the same rule and penalty.

It has been said of Thomas Paine that "he had no love for old mistakes nor admiration for ancient lies," and to that great man's leadership, I whole-heartedly subscribe.

Chapter XV.

The Virgin Birth, or Mary,
The Holy Ghost, Joseph and Jesus.

In a public debate with the Reverend Charles Francis Potter on the question of the "Virgin Birth of Christ," the Reverend John Roach Straton, before a crowded audience in Carnegie Hall[12] read the details of the birth of Christ as recorded in the book of St. Matthew of the New Testament.

In reading the description of the birth of Christ before this public gathering I maintain that the Reverend Mr. Straton insulted not only the moral sensibilities of the people who heard him, but also their mental sensibilities, when he exposed his monumental ignorance in accepting this narrative as the truth. I venture to say, if the Reverend John Roach Straton were to detail the birth of any other person in the same language which was used relative to Christ, his audience would have rebuked this insult in the unmistakable terms of hoots and hisses. No less a person than the Reverend John Haynes Holmes, in a public statement, has characterized this narrative as obscene.

From the pulpit of Calvary Baptist Church, of which Reverend John Roach Straton is pastor, the Reverend W. L. Pettingill, as reported in the New York Sun of December 4, 1923, said this:

"Only those who believe in Christ as God, in His Virgin Birth and in His Resurrection in the body -- the irreducible minimum of the Christian faith -- will go to heaven. Those who deny any or all of these tenets will be lost -- they will go to hell."

"We have got to smoke them out," cried the reverend, and when he made this last statement I suppose he forgot for the moment that he was not living in the days when thousands suffered death by fire and fagot for denying the very things that he now demands that we all accept. If the ecclesiastical arm were as strong now as it was then, how sweet would the "smoke" of my flesh be to the nostrils of the Reverend Mr. Pettingill. What this reverend gentleman said further particularly interests us at this moment.

"These things do not permit of interpretation. There is no altering the words written. Either the Virgin Birth is truth, or two things must be -- the Bible must be false in regard to this or Jesus of Nazareth was a bastard. Either Jesus was God or a hideous impostor." [Italics Mine.]

---

[12] March 22, 1924.

I reject the Virgin Birth as Biblically related, Reverend Mr. Pettingill, and accept the alternative.

That Jesus was a hideous impostor has been conclusively proven by others. As we are not concerned with his imposture in this book, we cannot go into details of that element of his deception. We are concerned with his illegitimacy, and to that end we will continue; although in doing so I will be acting contrary to the attitude of a celebrated author, who, when asked during an address before the students of a prominent college what he thought of Christianity, replied: "I am not interested in Jewish family scandals."

I quote the Gospel according to St. Matthew, Chapter 1, Verse 18.

18. Now the birth of Jesus Christ was on this wise: When as his mother Mary was espoused to Joseph, before they came together, she was found with child of the Holy Ghost.

The inference here is too plain for even a dullard not to understand. A young girl is betrothed to a young man. Mind you, not to a "holy ghost"; not to something intangible and unseen, but to a young man, virile and in possession of all his faculties. "Before they came together," which needs no elucidation, the girl was found to be "with child." Now the writer of this narrative was fully aware of the fact that before a child is born it is necessary for a man and a woman to "come together."

Laying aside the pertinency of a child asking an explanation of what is meant by "coming together," we see the necessary male adjunct of this union by the introduction of the Holy Ghost. In claiming that it was the Holy Ghost who cohabited with Mary and was the father of Jesus, Elbert Hubbard thought it was the greatest compliment ever paid to man.

I say this solemnly and with deep conviction: If all the acts of adultery and unfaithfulness could be blamed upon the Holy Ghost and accepted as such by the injured party, a great deal of misery and sorrow of the world would be avoided. Men are so jealous of their loved ones, that if they find them liberal even with their glances and smiles to other men, a situation hard to overcome presents itself. What, I pray you, would be the result of the situation in which we find Mary, the espoused of Joseph and mother of Jesus? I am sure the Holy Ghost story would not hold water. I am sure the young man would say: "If you are unfaithful to me before we are married, what can I expect after we are wedded?" I am inclined to think the young man would say that he was "finished with her" and would demand the return of his diamond ring. More than one proposed marriage has been broken for a far less cause than that of finding the espoused "with child."

Men are very adverse to supporting other men's children. As each man, in a situation of this kind, is a law unto himself, we will proceed with the story as it concerns Joseph.

St. Matthew, Chapter 1, Verse 19.

19. Then Joseph her husband, being a just man, and not willing to make her a public example, was minded to put her away privily.

Bully for Joseph! His act is commendable. Surely worthy of our praise. But why "put her away privily"? And why was he not willing "to make her a public example"? Why was he not jubilant that God complimented him to such an extent that he chose his sweetheart to bear his son and Savior of the world?

It is quite evident from the narrative that Joseph bore a great love for Mary and was willing to marry her despite the fact that she had slipped from the path of virtue even after her betrothal to him.

That some sly and smooth-tongued seducer was responsible for Mary's plight cannot be denied. A super Don Juan he must have been to be able to entice a girl already pledged to another to suffer his embrace.

And although it is claimed by some that Pandora, a "good for nothing" neighbor, was responsible for Mary's condition, the time is far too distant for the production of any credible evidence regarding the notorious affair, as evidence in such cases is considered the most difficult to secure. "Then Joseph her husband, being a just man, and not willing to make her a public example, was minded to put her away privily," is sufficient evidence alone to brand Mary's condition with the stamp of unfaithfulness.

No doubt the parents of Mary, to avoid having a public scandal and to check the vile tongue of Mrs. Grundy, pleaded with Joseph to take Mary to a place where they were unknown until after the delivery of the child. Such a thing is done now, and there is no reason to suppose that it wasn't done then. No doubt Mary herself was anxious to repent, and in her pleadings with Joseph must have promised him -- faithfully -- that she would never again stray from the path of virtue and rectitude. Joseph evidently believed with Shakespeare, "that love is not love that alters when it alteration finds," and so he overlooked the slight "alteration" he found in Mary. If the angel of the Lord could tell Joseph about the Holy Ghost, he could surely inform him what Shakespeare was to write more than 1,500 years hence!

But despite his great love for Mary and despite her "slight alteration" Joseph began to have his doubts about the Holy Ghost version of her condition as the narrative continues.

St. Matthew, Chapter 1, Verse 20.

20. But while he thought on these things, behold, the angel of the Lord appeared unto him in a dream, saying, Joseph, thou son of David, fear not to take unto thee Mary thy wife: for that which is conceived in her is of the Holy Ghost.

One thing the above quotation proves. It proves that Joseph did not believe that the child conceived by Mary was of the Holy Ghost. Joseph gave the matter serious consideration.

And if Joseph, who was on the scene and acquainted with all the facts of the deed, did not believe the "ghost story" how can you expect us, after nearly two thousand years have elapsed, to accept it as a verity? As for having the truth revealed to him in a dream by an angel, that is too laughable for mention. Truly that is "such stuff as dreams are made of."

That the story of Christ and his so-called virgin birth is a pure fabrication and myth, and was invented by the deluded and superstitious believers of that time, is attested to by the following verses of the narrative. It was an attempt on the part of some to "contest or reinterpret" the "first will" or Old Testament, in an endeavor that they might become the favored ones of God. The text proves unequivocally that it was not the miraculous birth of Christ that was of so much concern; the supreme importance was the fulfillment of the so-called prophecy that "a virgin shall conceive and bear a son"; as the following text proves.

St. Matthew, Chapter 1, Verses 21-25.

21. And she shall bring forth a son, and thou shalt call his name JESUS: for he shall save his people from their sins.

22. Now all this was done, that it might be fulfilled which was spoken of the Lord by the prophet, saying,

23. Behold, a virgin shall be with child, and shall bring forth a son, and they shall call his name Emmanuel, which being interpreted is, God with us.

24. Then Joseph being raised from sleep did as the angel of the Lord had bidden him, and took unto him his wife:

25. And knew her not till she had brought forth her firstborn son: and he called his name JESUS.

It is unnecessary for me to show the falsity of the prophecy, "now all this was done, that it might be fulfilled which was spoken of the Lord by the prophet, saying:

"Behold, a virgin shall be with child, and shall bring forth a son, and they shall call his name Emmanuel; which being interpreted is, God with us," because Thomas Paine has so admirably unmasked this monstrous lie, I am going to quote his version of it from his celebrated "Age of Reason."[13]

"Behold a virgin shall conceive, and bear a son," Isaiah, chap. vii. ver. 14, has been interpreted to mean the person called Jesus Christ, and his mother Mary, and has been echoed through Christendom for more than a thousand years; and such has been the rage of this opinion that scarcely a spot in it but has been stained with blood, and marked with desolation in consequence of it. Though it is not my intention to enter into controversy on subjects of this kind, but to confine myself to show that the Bible is spurious, and thus, by taking away the foundation, to overthrow at once the whole structure of superstition raised thereon, I will, however, stop a moment to expose the fallacious application of this passage.

Whether Isaiah was playing a trick with Ahaz, king of Judah, to whom this passage is spoken, is no business of mine; I mean only to show the misapplication of the passage, and that it has no more reference to Christ and his mother than it has to me and my mother. The story is simply this: The king of Syria and the king of Israel, (I have already mentioned that the Jews were split into two nations, one of which was called Judah, the capital of which was Jerusalem, and the other Israel), made war jointly against Ahaz, king of Judah, and marched their armies toward Jerusalem. Ahaz and his people became alarmed, and the account says, verse 2, *"And his heart was moved, and the heart of his people, as the trees of the wood are moved with the wind."*

In this situation of things, Isaiah addresses himself to Ahaz, and assures him in the *name of the Lord* (the cant phrase of all the prophets) that these two kings should not succeed against him; and to satisfy Ahaz that this should be the case, tells him to ask a sign. This, the account says, Ahaz declined doing, giving as a reason that he would not tempt the Lord; upon which Isaiah, who is the speaker, says, ver. 14, "Therefore the Lord himself shall give you a sign, *Behold, a virgin shall conceive and bear a son*"; and the 16th verse says, "*For before this child shall know to refuse the evil, and choose the good,* the land that thou abhorrest, (or dreadest, meaning Syria and the kingdom of Israel) shall be forsaken of both her kings." Here then was the sign, and the time limited for the completion of the assurance or promise, namely, before this child should know to refuse the evil and choose the good.

Isaiah having committed himself thus far, it became necessary to him, in order to avoid the imputation of being a false prophet and the consequence thereof, to take measures to make this sign appear. It certainly was not a difficult thing, in any time of the world, to find a girl with child, or to make her so, and perhaps Isaiah knew of one beforehand; for I do not suppose that the prophets of that day were any more to be trusted than the priests of this. Be that, however, as it may,

---

[13] "Age of Reason," pages 122-124.

he says in the next chapter, ver. 2, "And I took unto me faithful witnesses to record, Uriah the priest, and Zechariah the son of Jeberechiah, and *I went unto the prophetess, and she conceived and bare a son.*"

Here, then, is the whole story, foolish as it is, of this child and this virgin; and it is upon the barefaced perversion of this story, that the book of Matthew, and the impudence and sordid interests of priests in later times, have founded a theory which they call the Gospel; and have applied this story to signify the person they call Jesus Christ, begotten, they say, by a ghost, whom they call holy, on the body of a woman, engaged in marriage, and afterward married, whom they call a virgin, 700 years after this foolish story was told; a theory which, speaking for myself, I hesitate not to disbelieve, and to say, is as fabulous and as false as God is true.[14]

But to show the imposition and falsehood of Isaiah, we have only to attend to the sequel of this story, which, though it is passed over in silence in the book of Isaiah, is related in the 28th chapter of the second Chronicles, and which is, that instead of these two kings failing in their attempt against Ahaz, king of Judah, as Isaiah had pretended to foretell in the name of the Lord, they succeeded; Ahaz was defeated and destroyed, a hundred and twenty thousand of his people were slaughtered, Jerusalem was plundered, and two hundred thousand women, and sons and daughters, carried into captivity. Thus much for this lying prophet and imposter, Isaiah, and the book of falsehoods that bears his name.

I challenge every minister of Christianity to refute Thomas Paine's exposure of this all too monstrous lie and the most dastardly piece of imposition ever perpetrated upon the human race! I make no restrictions to this challenge. It includes every gentleman of the cloth of every church professing the Christian doctrine.

Prove Thomas Paine false or cease your hypocrisy with its unholy gain!

---

[14] In the 14th verse of the 7th chapter, it is said that the child should be called Immanuel; but this name was not given to either of the children otherwise than as a character which the word signifies. That of the prophetess was called Maher-shalal-hash-baz, and that of Mary was called Jesus.

Chapter XVI

The Birth of Jesus Christ
According to The Gospel of St. Luke

Perhaps the birth of Christ as related by St. Matthew was not minute and conclusive enough as to the details of the sexual act and so we turn to the Gospel of St. Luke to supply this most interesting account.

As we have already reviewed cases of unfaithfulness, incest, polygamy, prostitution, rape, adultery, child by whoredom, and almost every phase of immorality known to man, it will not, I am sure, be inappropriate to continue with this version of the birth of Christ.

I quote The Gospel According to St. Luke, Chapter 1, Verses 26-28.

26. And in the sixth month the angel Gabriel was sent from God unto a city of Galilee, named Nazareth,

27. To a virgin espoused to a man whose name was Joseph, of the house of David; and the virgin's name was Mary.

28. And the angel came in unto her, and said, Hail, thou that art highly favoured, the Lord is with thee: blessed art thou among women.

One difference already noted between the narrative of St. Matthew and St. Luke regarding Mary and the conception of her child, is that in St. Matthew it is the Holy Ghost who is responsible for her pregnant condition and in St. Luke the angel Gabriel is mentioned. And although here is a distinct contradiction between the two accounts, the designation of the character by different names responsible for the condition makes very little real difference. What we are concerned with is the fact that it was someone else than the man she had promised to wed.

We have read of angels "whispering" to a person, but we have never heard of an instance where "the angel came in unto her." And the word Angel is equally appropriate as that of the Holy Ghost.

The Gospel according to St. Luke, Chapter 1, Verse 29.

29. And when she saw him, she was troubled at his saying, and cast in her mind what manner of salutation this should be.

Ah! We have the secret direct from the Bible. Let me repeat the above quotation to bring its full significance to you. "And when she saw *him,* she was troubled at *his* saying, and cast in her mind what manner of salutation this should be." I wonder what this *he* angel proposed to Mary

129

that made her "cast in her mind what manner of salutation this should be"? Is it possible that she was innocent of the relationship he proposed, or was she simply amazed at his daring and boldness? especially so, since she was already engaged to some one else and was mindful of her virginity. And what an altogether different story it would have been if God had sent a she angel to visit Mary! To my mind a woman is a nearer approach to an angel than a man could ever be.

No wonder the poor girl was troubled. She had a difficult problem on her hands. Although the Bible is not explicit in what this *he* angel said to Mary, we are not devoid of imagination; and so continue.

The Gospel According to St. Luke, Chapter 1, Verse 30.

30. And the angel said unto her, Fear not, Mary: for thou hast found favour with God.

From this verse we glean the manner of pursuit and what the angel was after. "Fear not" is the pet phrase of the seducer. The angel's courting has not been in vain. Victory has been achieved. Similar action to that of Mary is taking place, at this very moment, throughout the world. Seduction, unfortunately, is still too commonly prevalent. Is it possible that the angel "doped" Mary as sometimes happens in cases of this kind and when she "awoke" she was unaware of what had transpired? For she says,

The Gospel According to St. Luke, Chapter 1, Verse 34.

34. Then said Mary unto the angel, How shall this be, seeing I know not a man?

You see Mary was aware of the fact that without a man's help she could not have a child. Where Mary received her sex education I do not know; perhaps from the story of Tamar and Judah? And so we continue with the unusual story of the intercourse of an angel with a maid.

The Gospel According to St. Luke, Chapter 1, Verse 31.

31. And, behold, thou shalt conceive in thy womb, and bring forth a son, and shalt call his name JESUS.

Yes, the deed is done. The angel has satisfied his desire. The prophecy is well founded. As truly "prophetic" as Isaiah and his subsequent action. Although any potent man could accomplish the same result. For more of this kind of "literature" continue the narrative as it consecutively appears in the Bible.

But it occurs to me that if Jesus was to be immaculately conceived, and God was to be his father, he should have chosen a different place of incubation than that of a woman's womb. It is in the womb that all of us mortals are conceived and the Bible's own testimony regarding this birth is rather disconcerting to those devout believers in the miraculous birth of Christ. If there were to be a really and truly miraculous birth, conception should have taken place in the ear, or arm, or leg, but in the womb -- never!

It is quite probable that a story like the one just related, detailed in any other book than the Bible, would be construed as being of a highly spicy tone and condemned as being vicious in its moral conclusion. Surely, Mary would be looked upon as a girl whose character was not worthy of emulation. Her actions indicate that a knowledge of sex would have been very helpful, because her ignorance was certainly not bliss. I wish for the moment to speak to the fathers and mothers of young girls; particularly those of the Christian faith. What would you say if your daughter came and told you that she was "with child by an angel"? What would the young man to whom she was engaged in marriage say about her condition? I am sure you would immediately make a thorough search for this angel and bring him to account. In certain parts of this country, this angel, if caught, would not be given much of an opportunity to explain himself. And if he said that he was "an angel of the Lord" you know how much weight that would have.

And now you parents, you who are so anxious about the welfare of your daughter, and so mindful of her amusements and companions; if your daughter were reading a book, whose plot corresponded to the story of Mary, would you not admonish her that such a book was unfit to be read, that its example was vicious and detrimental, and that "nothing good" can come from such stories? Wouldn't you make an effort to discourage her interest in such literature? By what rule, then, does a story which is suggestive in any other book, become of high moral value when it is found in the Bible?

Now let me say a word about the moral import of this narrative. It is of the grossest obscenity. It poisons the minds of children not only to the vital facts of biological science, but even prejudices the minds of adults to these vital facts. Would you think of reading this story to your children for the purpose of drawing a moral lesson? What moral principle can be inculcated from this narrative? Is it the seduction of Mary and the illegitimacy of Christ?

Chapter XVII.

Elisabeth, the Cousin of Mary,
Zacharias and the Angel Gabriel

It is generally true, that when a thief visits a community, more than one person suffers a loss before the thief is caught. The same can be said of impostors who prey upon others for existence; seldom do they stop with one victim. And it is equally true that the seducer rarely dishonors one woman only. Since the Bible would not be conclusive and complete without a story of seduction, we will proceed with the next narrative.

What impresses us in that which is to follow, is not so much the seduction of a woman -- this we recorded in the previous chapter -- as the fact that one woman was not sufficient to satisfy the desires of God! His "holy ghost" and "angel" sought and consummated intimate relations with two women; and curiously, these women were closely related, being by blood first cousins -- peculiarly a family affair. Why these two women were especially selected is not revealed. For very strangely one was a virgin and the other a married woman "well stricken in years," who presumably had passed her menopause, but whom, like Cleopatra, evidently "age cannot wither, nor time stale her infinite variety."

One thing is certain, Elisabeth's age did not dampen the ardor of this potent male -- this profligate and seducing angel.

I cannot say for certain that it was the same angel of the Lord who was responsible for the impregnation of both Mary and Elisabeth, but as I have no conclusive evidence to the contrary, I think the circumstances are such as to lead one to believe that it was the one and the same angel. I have presumed to accept it as such.

If through the instrumentality of one angel God was unable to satisfy his desires, and chose to use two angels, then I stand subject to correction. One particular and pertinent difference, however, between the seduction of Mary and that of Elisabeth, is, that Mary was only betrothed in marriage, while Elisabeth was already bound by law and ceremony.

In the case of Mary, she still had time to change her mind as to who was to be her husband and the father of her child. This we all agree is the right and prerogative of every girl. If a young lady, while engaged to a young man, should meet another young man, whom she likes better and whom she thinks will make her a better husband and is better suited to be the father of her children, decides to change her mind, she should certainly be privileged to "break her engagement" and accept the man she prefers.

But in the case of Elisabeth, we are dealing with a lady already married. She had already pledged faithfulness, to the end of her days, to the man to whom she was married, and only by a divorce could she become free of her sacred pledge and marriage bond in order that she might, morally, have marital relations with another man.

We all admire constancy and loyalty. These two virtues are cherished by all. If a woman no longer finds favor in her husband; no longer finds the love she craves, the proper thing to do is to separate. The same rule applies to the husband. But to violate the pledge of loyalty while still married is abhorred the world over, and has ever been -- in every age and in every clime -- God, Angels and Holy Ghosts to the contrary, notwithstanding.

"Free love" may be a spiritual code, but as yet the human race has not voiced its approval of it.

As most marriages, after the legal formalities are complied with, are consummated by a religious ceremony, and the final oaths administered when the bride and groom, hand in hand, place them upon the Bible as a seal of divine approval to their union, let us look into the Bible for its code and instructions and examples of this sacred institution, truly this holy union -- Marriage.

The Gospel According to St. Luke, Chapter 1, Verses 5-7.

5. There was in the days of Herod, the king of Judea, a certain priest named Zacharias, of the course of Abia: and his wife was of the daughters of Aaron, and her name was Elisabeth.

6. And they were both righteous before God, walking in all the commandments and ordinances of the Lord blameless.

7. And they had no child, because that Elisabeth was barren; and they both were now well stricken in years.

The significant thing in the above quotation is that both Zacharias and Elisabeth had kept inviolate their marriage vows. Never had either of them broken faith with the other. Their love and companionableness for each other prevailed throughout their lives and as "they both were now well stricken in years," would it not have been a glorious thing had the Bible revealed to us the secret or code by which they lived their lives, so that we poor mortals could fashion ours upon it? If Zacharias and Elisabeth knew the secret of a perfect union, why didn't the Bible reveal it to us? Oh! how precious that knowledge would be to the human race!

134

The Bible reveals a "secret" to us, but is it the secret we want revealed?

The Gospel According to St. Luke, Chapter 1, Verses 8-12.

8. And it came to pass, that, while he executed the priest's office before God in the order of his course,

9. According to the custom of the priest's office, his lot was to burn incense when he went into the temple of the Lord.

10. And the whole multitude of the people were praying without at the time of incense.

11. And there appeared unto him an angel of the Lord standing on the right side of the altar of incense.

12. And when Zacharias saw him, he was troubled, and fear fell upon him.

Certainly the Angel could not have selected a better time or place to speak to Zacharias than at the temple where he was "laboring in behalf of the Lord."

"And when Zacharias saw *him,* he was troubled and fear fell upon him."

It is quite apparent from the narrative that old Zacharias must have been familiar with this *he* angel's intentions. For why should a "servant of the Lord" fear a visit from "an angel of the Lord"? I should think he would be quite jubilant over the occasion.

The Gospel According to St. Luke, Chapter 1, Verses 13-17.

13. But the angel said unto him, Fear not, Zacharias; for thy prayer is heard; and thy wife Elisabeth shall bear thee a son, and thou shalt call his name John.

14. And thou shalt have joy and gladness; and many shall rejoice at his birth.

15. For he shall be great in the sight of the Lord, and shall drink neither wine nor strong drink; and he shall be filled with the Holy Ghost, even from his mother's womb.

16. And many of the children of Israel shall he turn to the Lord their God.

135

17. And he shall go before him in the spirit and power of Elias, to turn the hearts of the fathers to the children, and the disobedient to the wisdom of the just; to make ready a people prepared for the Lord.

Here again is the pet phrase of the seducer. "Fear not, Zacharias -- thy wife Elisabeth shall bear *thee* a son." But so far as I am able I can find no expressed desire on the part of either Zacharias or Elisabeth to have a son. And if we remember well the narrative, Zacharias was "well stricken in years" from which we are to infer that he was no longer able physically to perform the act necessary to make him a father.

Is there any wonder that old Zacharias was *troubled* by the visit of this *he* angel, especially when he was told to "fear not, thy wife Elisabeth shall bear thee a son"?

The Gospel According to St. Luke, Chapter 1, Verse 18.

18. And Zacharias said unto the angel, Whereby shall I know this? for I am an old man, and my wife well stricken in years.

Surely this was a proper question. Zacharias knew full well that he was unable to bring about the condition this *he* angel predicted, and naturally inquired how the accomplishment would be effected.

"What a fool this old man is," this *he* angel must have cynically muttered to himself. But to old Zacharias, the Bible tells us, he said something quite different.

The Gospel According to St. Luke, Chapter 1, Verse 19.

19. And the angel answering said unto him, I am Gabriel, that stand in the presence of God; and am sent to speak unto thee, and to shew thee these glad tidings.

Could a schoolboy miss the point? Why, I, Gabriel, am to perform this noble deed. Churchmen always surround themselves with the hypocrisy of being "messengers of the Lord," and in doing so they come pretty close to getting everything they want.

If this condition was to come about by the desire of God, why didn't he tell Zacharias about it himself without the necessity of an intermediary he angel? God spoke to Abraham and Moses and other Biblical characters, and I see no good reason why he shouldn't have spoken directly to Zacharias.

The Gospel According to St. Luke, Chapter 1, Verse 20.

20. And, behold, thou shalt be dumb, and not able to speak, until the day that these things shall be performed, because thou believest not my words, which shall be fulfilled in their season.

Poor old Zacharias! What chance did he have with this passionate and robust *he* angel? No doubt he thought "discretion is the better part of valor" and kept his mouth shut while the seduction went merrily on.

What else could he do but remain dumb? Wouldn't such an encounter and such a threat make any *old* man speechless? And by the way, if Zacharias did not believe that this *he* angel was sent by God do you know of any reason why we should? Zacharias was acquainted with the gentleman and certainly he should have known who he was.

The Gospel According to St. Luke, Chapter 1, Verses 21-23.

21. And the people waited for Zacharias, and marvelled that he tarried so long in the temple.

22. And when he came out, he could not speak unto them: and they perceived that he had seen a vision in the temple; for he beckoned unto them, and remained speechless.

23. And it came to pass, that, as soon as the days of his ministration were accomplished, he departed to his own house.

So much for Zacharias, and now a word about his wife, Elisabeth. What was her attitude in the matter? In a way she was more concerned about the affair than her husband. She had to bear the child. Did she encourage the angel? Or did the angel see her first and did she tell him to tell Zacharias to keep his mouth shut, "until the day that these things shall be performed ... which shall be fulfilled in their season"?

And was old Zacharias speechless because he was warned by Elisabeth, as wives sometimes do, who carry on clandestine relations with other men? It is the consummation of "these things shall be performed" that interests us and so we continue.

The Gospel According to St. Luke, Chapter 1, Verses 24-25.

24. And after those days his wife Elisabeth conceived, and hid herself five months, saying,

25. Thus had the Lord dealt with me in the days wherein he looked on me, to take away my reproach among men.

Yes, the deed is done, for we read, "after those days his wife Elisabeth conceived, and hid herself five months." Nothing startling about that, except the hiding. It was to be expected that she would conceive. The result is in proper sequence to the act. The marvel or miracle, if you wish, would have been had she not conceived after the sexual relation with a potent man. Everything normal and in order as far as I can determine, except perhaps, for the act of adultery on the part of

Elisabeth, for we have Zacharias's own word that he could not do what "was fulfilled in their season."

Zacharias's own words, "for I am an old man" brands Elisabeth an adulteress. If Elisabeth was not guilty of faithlessness, why did she "hide herself five months"? It has been asked, and asked rightly: Whom was she hiding from? Certainly not from Zacharias, because he knew all about it. Did she hide herself, because the neighbors, knowing Zacharias's physical condition, would gossip? What do you think was the cause of Elisabeth's hiding?

"Thus has the Lord dealt with me in the days wherein he looked on me to take away my reproach among men." Lucky woman, is all that I can say, because from time immemorial the woman who in wedlock has borne a child from the seed of man other than her lawful husband, has felt the reproach of men until the end of her days.

Is this the part of the Bible women are strongly advised to follow? I strongly advise women against following the example of Elisabeth. If women do not heed my advice, and choose rather the authority of the Bible, they will soon find that men are not so credulous and people not so gullible as this narrative would have you believe. Only in the Bible are these things accepted and believed; they would not be tolerated in real life.

Before passing on to the next episode let me say a word to those who have their marriage solemnized by the Bible in a religious ceremony: and this to the blushing bride.

Is the action of Elisabeth in her relation with the angel and her attitude to poor old Zacharias the model that you are to fashion your wedded life upon?

Will you desert your husband, when "he is well stricken in years," for a younger and more virile man?

Will you willingly consent to an act of adultery with "an angel of the Lord"? Will you claim that the child in your womb is of the "Holy Ghost"? And hide yourself until it is all over?

Or will you be too loyal to your vows to even listen to the wooing words of a sly seducer?

And now just a word to the bridegroom: If you look forward to a happy married life, be sure before you make the young lady your wife, that she does not believe the Bible contains the proper moral code, and particularly that the story of Elisabeth will not be her guide in her life-companionship with you.

Chapter XVIII.

Jesus and the Sinner.

Far be it from me to question the acquaintances and companions of a person and least of all those of Jesus Christ. If Jesus chose to associate with women of questionable virtue and chastity surely he had a perfect right to do so. He is not the only one who has had such associates; but whether this choice was of his own free will or of necessity I do not know. But I do know this: Were I to write a story glorifying the prostitute; and accord to her the same social privileges; and act towards her with the same dignity; and place her upon the same level with virtuous women, there would rise a hue and cry from the religious forces that I was advocating "free love" and "undermining the foundation of the home"; and is it "spiritual righteousness" to have in your home a book detailing the scenes between a "woman of the street" -- a sinner, passionately displaying her attachment for a man while he is receiving the hospitality of another person, because this degrading scene is related in the Bible? As much as I sympathize with the prostitute; as much as I will do all in my power to alleviate the prejudice against her and help her to a worthy position in society, I strenuously object to her public performance of displaying her affection for Jesus as being fit material for the edification of our children.

Having in mind the adage that a person is known by the company he keeps, I will proceed with the Biblical narrative of Jesus and the Sinner.

I quote the Gospel according to St. Luke, Chapter 7, Verses 36-38.

36. And one of the Pharisees desired him that he would eat with him. And he went into the Pharisee's house, and sat down to meat.

37. And, behold, a woman in the city, which was a sinner, when she knew that Jesus sat at meat in the Pharisee's house, brought a alabaster box of ointment,

38. And stood at his feet behind him weeping, and began to wash his feet with tears, and did wipe them with the hairs of her head, and kissed his feet, and anointed them with the ointment.

Let us for the moment put ourselves in the position in which we find Jesus. What a compromising position it must have been to have a "sinner" (and the inference is only too plain) follow you about, enter the house where you are a guest, begin to inundate you with her tears, wash your feet and then wipe them with her hair, then kiss them, and finally annoint you with perfumed ointment! Mind you, after she had sprinkled his feet with tears and smothered them with kisses, she dries them with the silken tresses of her hair!

What more could any man receive? Surely the manifestation of a supreme love. No wonder she followed him about and only awaited the opportunity to show in an unmistakable manner her real affection for him.

What do you think of a man who allows a woman to do to him what this woman did to Jesus? Don't you think he could have been just as appreciative of her affection without this elaborate public display of washing, kissing, and anointing? Can you imagine Jesus after the washing he got and the anointing of the sweet-smelling ointment over him?

If Jesus did not object to artificial means of beautifying and making himself smell sweetly, what objection, I pray, can there be against the girls of to-day who devise means of artificially beautifying themselves? Didn't Jesus favor it? Didn't he like it? Then why shouldn't girls practise what Jesus himself was so much in favor of?

To those ministers who have so loudly denounced the girls of to-day and yet hold Jesus up as a model for mankind, I say, be consistent, ye hypocritical reformers. What was good enough for Jesus should certainly not be too vulgar for the girls of to-day. However, I would not advise any of our girls of to-day to do to the man they love what this woman did to Jesus. It is unbecoming not only to womankind, but is a mark of degeneration in a man.

In order to continue consecutively with the story I will quote the interpolated part between verses 38 to 44 of this chapter; for if these verses were not interpolated by some smart translator, who knew the effect this story would have upon thinking people, then they prove Jesus to have been the supreme hypocrite and impostor.

The Gospel According to St. Luke, Chapter 7, Verses 39-43.

39. Now when the Pharisee which had bidden him saw it, he spake within himself, saying, This man, if he were a prophet, would have known who and what manner of a woman this is that toucheth him; for she is a sinner.

40. And Jesus answering said unto him, Simon, I have somewhat to say unto thee. And he saith, Master, say on.

41. There was a certain creditor which had two debtors: the one owed him five hundred pence, and the other fifty.

42. And when they had nothing to pay, he frankly forgave them both. Tell me therefore, which of them will love him most?

142

43. Simon answered and said, I suppose that he, to whom he forgave most. And he said unto him, Thou has rightly judged.

This is pure camouflage, and does not in any way mitigate the nauseous washing, drying, kissing and anointing.

The Gospel According to St. Luke, Chapter 7, Verses 44-46.

44. And he turned to the woman, and said unto Simon, Seest thou this woman? I entered into thine house, thou gayest me no water for my feet: but she hath washed my feet with tears, and wiped them with the hairs of her head.

45. Thou gayest me no kiss: but this woman, since the time I came in, hath not ceased to kiss my feet.

46. My head with oil thou didst not anoint: but this woman hath anointed my feet with ointment.

Monumental conceit and the currying of favors from "women of the street" are attributes of the hero of Christianity upon which the leaders of this creed have failed to enlighten us. The insolence of Jesus in telling the man who had invited him to his home to partake of a meal with him, that this woman -- this sinner, mind you -- had washed his feet and wiped them with her hair and kissed and anointed them in the bargain, while he, his host, was guilty of such neglect, is without parallel.

Why, if I were Simon, I would have told Jesus that the function of washing one's feet is a personal task, and that if there were any woman of the street desirous of doing this service for him she should do it elsewhere. Simon would have been perfectly justified in making such a rejoinder.

And now for the climax of the episode.

The Gospel According to St. Luke, Chapter 7, Verses 47-48.

47. Wherefore I say unto thee, Her sins, which are many, are forgiven: for she loved much: but to whom little is forgiven, the same loveth little.

48. And he said unto her, Thy sins are forgiven.

Let me repeat the last line of the above quotation. "And he said unto her, Thy sins are forgiven." Now who wouldn't have forgiven her her sins for what she had done? Certainly she earned forgiveness. And the man would have been an ingrate had he not forgiven her. I would have forgiven the woman without the ministrations with which she attended Jesus.

It may be of interest to the reader to know that the Gospel according to St. Matthew records this scene somewhat differently. In the Gospel of St. Matthew it says that while Jesus was at meat with Simon, this woman of the street poured sweet-smelling ointment on his head, and the other guests objected to this lavish expenditure, because the ointment could be sold and the money given to the poor; which I think was a very sensible and commendable thought. To this proposal Jesus magnanimously replied: "Why trouble ye the woman? for she hath wrought a good work upon me. For ye have the poor always with you; but me ye have not always." I want this distinctly understood that it was the Son of God who was speaking!

Chapter XIX.

Conclusion.

As we concluded our review of the Old Testament while there still remained additional matter that was fit subject for our investigation; so we find the same condition prevailing in the New Testament. Enough subject matter still remains to be exposed; but were I to relate in detail all the vulgar sayings and repeat the indelicate expressions, I fear my task would never end.

Again I must say, the best evidence of the Bible's unworthiness lies in the Bible itself. To read it is sufficient to condemn it.

It is a tragedy to think that there are millions of people actually worshipping the Bible when the book is not fit even to receive their respect. I say this is a tragedy, because it shows the fearful ignorance and still more fearful superstition of a great portion of the living world, in an age of such marvelous scientific achievements and progress. Is it any wonder that the morality of mankind has not reached the heights man has achieved in other realms when we have such a spectacle as the following advertisement, "paid for by a native Pittsburgh Catholic business man who believes in his religion," which appeared in the New York Times, October 22, 1925?

Catholics Love the Bible

The Catholic Church cherishes the Bible. ALL OF IT. She believes the Bible to be the Word of God -- not a mere human document. She believes the Bible contains no errors. Catholics reverence the Bible so much that they rise and stand when it is read and KISS IT DEVOUTLY after reading it.

Ridicule or sympathy should be meted out to those who still accept the Bible as divine truth, when they have at their disposal the accumulated knowledge of the ages -- knowledge which not only proves the Bible to be false in every department in which it claims authority, but distinctly pernicious in its influence as well. If a man chooses to "kiss devoutly" the Bible, I pray that he will not force this humiliation upon his children.

We can only conclude that those who still accept the Bible as the infallible Word of God are so sadly deluded by superstition and fear that they haven't the courage and mental strength to throw off this paralyzing poison. But no matter for what cause, the time has come when such people should no longer be able to dictate to others in the intellectual and moral spheres of man.

If there were a real Bible for the human race, that book would contain all that this so-called Bible does not contain. The real Bible would begin with the alphabet and the multiplication table and contain every law and principle of nature. We would constantly consult its pages to determine our proper course through life. It would be our Guide and Enlightener. It would be the Text-book of our Existence; the Dictionary of our acts.

One thing is certain and beyond the peradventure of a doubt, and that is this: The real Bible would not contain the immoral stories that make up the major part of this fraudulent one. Why, Satan, if he existed, would loudly protest the charge that he was the author of such a shameful and degrading book as now bears the title of "Holy Scriptures." And mark this: In no other volume would this vulgar insult to the human race be tolerated.

Abraham Lincoln used the expression of "sinners calling the righteous to repentance"; and do we need a better illustration of the truth of it than in the statement of the Reverend George Elliott, editor of the "Methodist Review," a minister of the church and an advocate of the Bible's teachings, when he says in a protest against the books of to-day that "never in the history of American literature has it been so soiled by the stink of sex."[15]

---

[15] "Methodist Review," January-February, 1924.

Is it possible that the Reverend George Elliott has never read the Bible? Or is he like the little boy who was asked if he knew what was in the Bible and who replied, "Oh! yes; I know everything that's in it. Sister's young man's photo is in it, and ma's recipe for face cream, an' a lock of my hair cut off when I was a baby, an' the ticket for Pa's watch."

Where can you find another volume, Reverend George Elliott, that contains as many "sex stories" as does the Bible? If the story of "Lot and His Daughters" -- where a father is made drunk so his two virgin daughters may effect an incestuous union with him; and the story of "Tamar and her father-in-law Judah" -- where a daughter-in-law is with "child by whoredom" by her father-in-law; and the story of the "Rape of Tamar By Her Brother Amnon" -- a story where a loving and dutiful sister is outrageously ravished by her brother; if the adulterous episodes of David; the seduction of Mary, and the unfaithfulness of her cousin Elisabeth, do not "stink of sex," then pray what name would you give to their foul odor?

The time has come when the Bible must be stripped of all its false halos and be measured for what it actually is; and I make this prediction: when the Bible is considered in its true light, it will be relegated to a position of utter disrespect -- without foundation, not alone in fact, but in decency as well. For a clergyman to call the stories of other books obscene when he recommends the Bible, is like "the pot calling the kettle black." Instead of boasting of their connection with and support of the Bible, they should rightly hang their heads in shame.

On another occasion the Reverend Ralph W. Kohr,[16] writing to the editor and publisher of a popular magazine, had this to say concerning the stories it published.

"...is a dirty and suggestive publication coming pretty close to abuse of the legal use of the U.S. mails. It plays up the sexual passions and depicts the decadent and salacious tendencies in modern life. So far I suppose it is true to life, but life on its lower and baser side. It is destructive and subversive of what good remains in modern society, and helps give the car of modern civilization a further push down the road to ruin.

"I am thankful that there are a number of publishers in our fair land who would not be guilty of putting such a magazine on the market. As a man, and one who may consider himself a gentleman, I think the whole tone and moral influence of the publication is unworthy of you or any

---

[16] I have made repeated attempts to secure his address, and the church with which he is connected, but have been unable to do so. The editor in whose magazine his communication appeared, writes me as follows: "Replying to communication with further reference to Reverend Ralph W. Kohr's address, I regret to have to inform you that a diligent search of our files fails to reveal the information desired, and I cannot therefore comply with your request."

honorable person. Would you want your high-school daughter, if you have one, to read such trash?

"Burn the stuff and start a paper that has an ideal and is not lower even than the low average of many modern homes. Papers should not merely reflect life as it is, the petty and wicked phases of it, but should be constructive, helpful. Surely a publisher has a duty to society and a responsibility for the influence of the stories he permits to get into print. The tendency is downward, but that is no reason why it should be accelerated by exploitation."

More appropriate language, or a more truthful statement could not be made in characterizing the stories of the Bible, than the above letter, sent by the Reverend Ralph W. Kohr, to the editor of the magazine in question. Could there be "dirtier" and more suggestive stories than the ones we have just reproduced from the Bible? And could there be stories which come closer to the "abuse of the legal use of the United States mails?"

Have you ever read stories which played up the sexual passions and depicted the "salacious tendencies of life" better than the narratives we have just taken from the Bible? The stories we have quoted from the Bible "may be true to life," but surely "life on its lower and baser side." If such stories are "destructive and subversive of modern society and help give the car of modern civilization a further push down the road to ruin," then I cry that the Bible is the most destructive and subversive influence of modern civilization.

Lucky indeed are we that there are in this fair land of ours publishers who have not taken inspiration from the Bible in the kind of stories they supply to the public. Lucky, indeed, are we! And I wonder if the Bible, as clergymen are so boastful in maintaining, is the "best seller" because of its stories.

And if the Reverend Ralph W. Kohr considers himself a gentleman, then I consider the "whole tone and moral influence" of the Bible unworthy the support of any "honorable person." The Reverend Ralph W. Kohr asks this question and I use the same words in reference to the Bible: "Would you want your high-school daughter, if you have one, to read such trash?" Would you want your daughter, Reverend Ralph W. Kohr, if you have one, to read such trash as "Isaac and His Wife Rebekah," "The Rape of Dinah," "The Story of Esther," "Joseph and Potiphar's Wife," "Mary, Joseph and the 'Holy Ghost,'" "Elisabeth, Zacharias and Angel Gabriel" or any one of the salacious narratives from "Abram and Sarai" to "Jesus and the Sinner"?

If such literature as this is being blindly and madly circulated, then is it not time that some one who is not blind and some one who is not mad cry "Halt" to the further corruption of our children by the Bible? Or has the prophetic utterance of Shakespeare

"O, Judgment, thou art fled to brutish beasts
And men have lost their reason"

come to pass?

Is the Bible the book our daughter should read to become familiar with the Prince Charming of Life, that subtle magic that gives life a little bloom and a little sweetness? Should she read the Bible so as to fashion her life upon the acts of Sarai, or Potiphar's Wife, or Esther, or Mary, or Elisabeth? Should she read the Bible in the expectation that her lover, husband and life's companion should possess the "sterling" character of an Abraham, Isaac or a David?

If we give a child a book and tell that child in that book will be found "the key to happiness and duty," can we honestly and rightfully punish that child if he should follow the examples and precepts that the book contains?

If the Government sanctions the Bible, by giving exemption of taxation to the institutions that expound it, what a paradox it is to penalize those who are guilty of the very crimes which in the leaders of the Bible are condoned! Surely if David was pardoned by God for the crimes he committed, and we are told that David "was a man after God's own heart," should we not pardon those guilty of the same crimes that David committed? And what hypocrisy it is on the part of our Government to have the Bible in our courts of law for the culprit to take his oath upon and then be tried for the very crimes which the Bible itself sanctions. Is the blindness of the Statue of Justice to be taken as literally true -- because this travesty and parody of justice continues day after day?

Could there be a more ludicrous situation than this? Recently I attended the court session of a man being tried for rape. In taking the stand in his own behalf the man was given the Bible to place his hand upon and made to take an oath "that he would tell the truth, the whole truth and nothing but the truth, so help me God," and yet in that very Bible is recorded one of the most heartrending cases of rape known to man!

Since we are instructed to read the Bible for our "key to happiness and duty," is it not reasonable to suppose that the reading of the Bible prompted this act of rape? And is it not also reasonable to suppose that ministers of the gospel, whose profession has supplied perpetrators of every crime on the calendar, from petty larceny and disorderly conduct to rape and murder, are prompted in their acts by the reading of the Bible? Shades of Father Hans Schmidt and Pastor Richardson!

And my reasonableness to suppose this, comes from the fact that the greatest number of inmates in our penal institutions are those who have received Biblical instruction. So great an authority as Havelock Ellis, in his masterful book, "The Criminal"[17] makes this statement: "In all countries religion, or superstition, is closely related to crime."

And why should it be otherwise, when it is not our relation to our fellow-men that will save our "souls" but "by grace are ye saved thru faith; and that not of ourselves."[18] And "without shedding of blood is no emission."[19] And "He that believeth and is baptised shall be saved; but he that believeth not shall be damned."[20]

Do we need a better illustration of religious homicidal mania, induced by Bible reading, than the case reported in the New York Times, November 28, 1924:

---

[17] Page 185.
[18] Ephesians, 2:8.
[19] Hebrews, 9:22.
[20] Mark, 16:16.

Crazed by Religion, Maid With Axe Kills One and Gashes Two.

This was the case of a woman who brutally killed her employer, fatally injured his wife, and wounded their daughter, who attempted to intercede in their behalf. When arrested for the crime and subjected to examination by the police, the woman said, *"Why should I be sorry when the Lord told me to do it?"* But a few months before this horrible crime the world was appalled and shocked by the burning to death of three members of a man's family because of his delusion that the "Holy Ghost" had whispered to him that only "through fire" could he purge his soul of sin. And let us not forget the brutal murder of a crippled father by a mother and daughter, who, after listening to a revivalist at a Bible meeting, "heard the voice of God," went to their home, and murdered the old man while he lay helpless in bed.

Let me recall a case as reported in the *New York Times* of April 27, 1922. John Cornyn, of San Francisco, shot and killed his two boys, one seven and the other eight, because, according to the police, he had been in "communication" with his wife who had been dead a year and she had asked him to "send all of her five children to her."[21]

It is not generally known that Charles J. Guiteau, the assassin of President Garfield, was a devout religious believer, and was engaged in writing a book, entitled, "The Truth a Companion to the Bible," when he was inspired by God to commit this dastardly crime against the Republic by the murder of the President.[22]

And in the *New York American,* August 20, 1925, appears this tragic item:

Kills Her Baby in Crib at
Angel's Call

Amityville Woman Stabs Sleeping Infant
with Table Knife to "Send
It To Heaven."

Did the reading of the story of the sacrifice of Isaac by his father Abraham prompt this poor deluded woman to murder her child?

And yet we have certain judges, suspending sentences upon culprits only upon condition that they attend church and read the Bible! I could cite instances of this kind to fill an entire volume, but merely refer you to the daily newspapers to supply this information. And now, if you will, let me quote an item which shows the "direful" result of those who

---

[21] Quoted from "A Magician Among the Spirits," by Houdini. Page 182.
[22] "A Magician Among the Spirits," Page 188.

"have no religion" and are minus "that great consolation that comes from a belief in the saving grace of Christ."

I quote from the New York Evening Mail of November 16, 1921:

There are two institutions that Walcott, Iowa, the richest town per capita in Iowa, prides itself in not possessing. These are churches and jails. In its religious beliefs, Walcott is unique. For more than fifty years the town has been without a church. It once had a jail, but like its only church, established sixty-five years ago and which existed but a few years, it was put in the discard. While the jail building stands, there is no vestige of a church edifice. But there are no locks to the jail, and the hinges have rotted off. "We are freethinkers and believe in free American citizenship seven days a week. We do not need preachers to dictate to us. We are better off without them," states Mayor Strohbeen, in expressing Walcott's lack of churches. "We are getting along very well as we are -- much better than with churches. We like to be let alone. There is no more peaceful or law-abiding town in the United States than Walcott. Why should we want churches? They bring strife and dissension -- we want peace and quietude," commented the town's popular mayor. In a business and commercial way Walcott is a thriving town. It has two banks with combined deposits of $1,500,000. This is a remarkable showing when it is considered that the population of the town is but 384. It has a consolidated school -- second to none in this part of the state. Recently the citizens erected a fine auditorium. There Chautauquas and musical entertainments are held on week days and dances on Sundays.

Since the appearance of this item in the newspapers, I am informed that the religious forces of nearby towns have contributed enough money to erect a church. The building of the jail will have to be done at the town's expense.

But let us get back to our subject and the Reverend Ralph W. Kohr, while I tell him that not only are the Bible's stories unfit to be read by our daughters, but I will go a step farther and say, that the children sent to Sunday School to have the Bible expounded to them and to be inculcated with a reverence for it as being the Word of God are being tainted with utter stupidity and degrading superstition.

If the Bible contained only the trash that the Reverend in his letter to the editor said that his magazine contained, then the Bible would be only as "trashy" as that magazine; but as it is, the Bible contains matter a thousand times more harmful and pernicious. One thing is certain, this editor does not claim that the stories appearing in his magazine are touched by divine inspiration.

If corruption in one instance is punishable by law, then contamination by any other method should meet the same penalty. If bastardy, adultery, prostitution, rape, and incest are unfit subjects for our

152

children, the title of "Holy Bible" upon the covers of a book, cannot, magic-like, transform these immoralities into cultural virtues!

And the following letter written by Mark Twain, in answer to a protest of a young woman superintendent in the Children's Department of the Brooklyn Public Library, who charged that "Tom Sawyer" and "Huckleberry Finn" were corrupting the morals of the children, is indeed pertinent.[23]

"I am greatly troubled by what you say. I wrote Tom Sawyer and Huck Finn for adults exclusively, and it always distresses me when I find that boys and girls have been allowed access to them. The mind that becomes soiled in youth can never again be washed clean; I know this by my own experience, and to this day I cherish an unappeasable bitterness against the unfaithful guardians of my young life, who not only permitted but compelled me to read an unexpurgated Bible through before I was 15 years old. None can do that and ever draw a clean, sweet breath again this side of the grave. Ask that young lady -- she will tell you so.

"Most honestly do I wish I could say a softening word or two in defense of Huck's character, since you wish it, but really in my opinion it is no better than those of Solomon, David, Satan, and the rest of the sacred brotherhood.

"If there is an unexpurgated [Bible] in the Children's Department, won't you please help that young woman remove Huck and Tom from that questionable companionship?"

"Burn the stuff and start a paper that has an ideal and is not lower even than the low average of many modern homes," cries the Reverend Mr. Kohr. I do not say "burn the Bible." I am not as bigoted as the Reverend Ralph W. Kohr about those things which I do not accept. I say preserve the Bible. Preserve it for the sake of exposure. Hold it high and flaunt it before all the people that its true worth may be known. Spread it far and wide, only do not contaminate our children with its contagiously vile pages. And again I make this prediction: When the Bible is once read and understood like other books, it will be rejected and discarded as being unfit and unworthy the attention and respect of man.

There is no home in America whose "low average" is lower than the morality found in the Bible. No home in America, no home in this great Republic of ours, should permit its sacred confines to be polluted by the presence of the Holy Scriptures.

---

[23] Mark Twain's Autobiography, Vol. 2, Page 335.

And what right has the Reverend Ralph W. Kohr to refer to "even the low average of many modern homes," when he is engaged in the distribution of the very book that may be responsible for the reduction of many modern homes to the low level of which he speaks? I dare say that if a modern volume were to be found in any home, containing the demoralizing stories that the Bible contains, the Reverend Ralph w. Kohr would become livid with rage and expostulate upon such a brazen disregard of modesty and the contamination of our lives with the "decadent and the salacious" element of life.

Do not burn any book. The greatest destroyer of falsehood is truth. Although truth at times appears lazy and apathetic it will eventually triumph. The searchlight of truth will burn falsehood with a fiercer intensity of destruction than the heat from the phosphorus flame.

Remember it is only in comparatively recent times that the glorious public schools were instituted to teach the people to read. And it will not be long before the believer in the Bible will be the exception rather than the rule. "Papers (books) should not merely reflect life as it is, the petty and wicked phases of it, but should be constructive, helpful." If the Reverend Ralph W. Kohr is an honest man, and these are his honest sentiments, then how is it possible for him to be a minister of the Bible? How can he be honest, and at the same time preach from the book which contains the stories we have recorded?

Does he call the recording of such phases of life "constructive and helpful," or are they more truthfully, "the petty and wicked part of it"? I am sure I do not need to explain their reflections of the pettiness and wickedness of life. Your own conscience tells you that! If as he says, "a publisher has a duty to society and a responsibility for the influence of the stories he permits to get into print," then surely the printers of the Bible are guilty of a monumental crime. And every man connected with its distribution and dissemination is equally guilty.

And if the tendency and impulse of life is downward, as he says, certainly "there is no reason why it should be accelerated by exploitation."

And now I ask you this pertinent question, Reverend Ralph W. Kohr, and *all* clergymen and ministers of religion: What right have *you* to exploit the Bible and prey upon the ignorant and credulous, when you know, measured for what it actually is, the Bible, as far as its stories are concerned, is not entitled to the respect of Man?

What right have you to exploit the Bible as the Word of God and wear the sanctimonious livery of a man of God, when the Bible has been shown to contain the most foul, repulsive, disgusting, licentious, repugnant, indecent, lascivious, wicked and corrupting episodes capable of performance by the vilest of beings? It is not necessary for me to tell you how vile and degrading is this so-called "Book of God." It is only too plainly evident to those who read it. Its stories, in their brazen disregard of modesty, prove my contention that they pollute the very pages upon which they are written. No greater fraud has been committed than to exploit the ignorant and the superstitious under the sanction that the Bible is the divinely inspired word of God and that "For God so loved the world, that he gave his only begotten Son, that whosoever believeth in him, should not perish, but have everlasting life."[24]

Until recently, I was told, the custom prevailing at the inauguration of some of our governors and Presidents, after the oath of office had been administered, was for the elected official to open the Bible and kiss a verse at random. The official would then mark the verse which he had kissed and give it to the press representatives to broadcast to the people.

This custom in part, however, has now been abandoned, for it is said that on one occasion the elected official kissed one of the verses of the Bible which, when marked and read, was discovered to be absolutely and positively filthy.

If an elected official now chooses to kiss the Bible at his inauguration (or her inauguration as in the case of "Ma" Ferguson of Texas, or Mrs. Nellie Ross of Wyoming) he either kisses the cover of the Bible, or a verse selected beforehand. In some cases a verse is merely indicated by placing a finger upon it.[25]

It is certainly an anomaly and an incongruity that there are verses in the Bible which cannot be mentioned separately and which are so grossly vile that extreme caution must be exercised so as to prevent their becoming public.

The sanction of the Bible in our Courts of Law, where a person is almost actually made to take an oath upon it before he is permitted to testify, is a travesty of justice.

The Bible itself, as a book of revealed truth, is a monumental lie!

Judges are continually complaining of the perjury of witnesses, and lawyers know only too well its prevalence. The oath, taken on the Bible, as now administered, is nothing but a formality. It has absolutely no restraining influence. The honest man will tell the truth irrespective of his oath upon the Bible, and the thief will lie, his oath upon the Bible

---

[24] John 3:16.
[25] At the first inauguration of Woodrow Wilson he opened the Bible at a specified chapter and "kissed it fervently." At the inauguration of Warren G. Harding he placed his finger on a selected text. Theodore Roosevelt merely placed his hand upon the Bible while the oath was administered. Both William Howard Taft and Calvin Coolidge kissed a page of the Bible without reference to any particular text (newspaper reports). The oath of office prescribed by the Constitution is purely secular, and does not call for the use of the Bible.

155

notwithstanding. The religious conviction of a person does not prevent him from violating his oath, nor does the unbelief of a person hinder him from performing his sacred duty to the fullest measure of integrity.

There is a case on record where a man was actually fined for sending a verse of the Bible openly through the mail! Just think of it. There are verses in the Bible which are too indecent to enjoy the privileges of the United States mail! -- verses which a Federal Court has officially condemned as being vile and vulgar, and in violation of the obscenity law.[26] (I call the attention of the Rev. Ralph W. Kohr to this situation.)

Is it possible? Is it really possible, that there are passages in the Bible which cannot be sent openly through the mail? Is it possible that God (and the religious elect solemnly swear that he wrote every word of the Bible) used obscene language in imparting his sacred knowledge to the world?

If this is true, and the records prove it to be true, this alone should be sufficient to condemn the Bible as a cultural book and destroy utterly the thought that it is the inspired word of God.

I could give the names of literally thousands of books that contain the very highest moral precepts which any one could open at any page and read any line and not have the slightest fear of shocking the tenderest sensibilities of a child.

And then again, why not use the Declaration of Independence, or more properly the Constitution of the United States, in the ceremony of inducting our officials into office? To swear upon the Bible allegiance to uphold the Constitution is a paradox, for the system of government as advocated in the Bible is the antithesis of our Republic, and the social order which it maintains is the direct contrary of the ideals of this great Democracy.

In some states, particularly in New York, where the Bible is permitted to be read in the public schools, the provision granting this privilege is generally stipulated in words to the effect: that upon the opening of school, a verse from the Bible, may be read "without note or comment."

Judging from the stipulation which is incorporated in the charters of the Boards of Education, it would appear that any verse in the Bible could be selected and read and that the one doing so would be performing his full duty. But nothing could be further from the truth. If any one dared to read some of the verses in the Bible, "without note or

---

[26] In 1895, John B. Wise, of Clay Center, Kansas, was arrested for sending obscene matter through the mails, which consisted wholly of a quotation from the Bible. In the United States Court, after a contest, he was found guilty and fined. -- Page 257, "Free Press Anthology," by Theodore Schroeder.

comment," he would be expelled from the school for grossly insulting the pupils.

It is amazing to me that so many people are ignorant of what the Bible actually contains. And it is still more amazing to me that educators, knowing what the Bible contains (for surely they know as much about the Bible as I do), permit this outrageous performance of reading the Bible to our public school children, to continue day after day. As educators, it is their duty to protest against this insult to the intelligence of the people and to the educational system of this country. To permit the Bible to be read daily to our public school children and to impress upon their tender minds a reverence for it as the infallible word of God, is to me not only a dereliction of duty which should be censured in the severest of terms, but is positively criminal. As I wish to avoid any interference with the distribution of my book I will refrain from quoting those verses which the Court has condemned as being obscene, but which nevertheless deserve to be exposed to the pitiless rays of the light of day.

"But if you take away our Bible, what will you give us in exchange," is the cry of the stupid and ignorant. If we eradicate fear, prejudice, hatred and superstition from the human mind, must we replace them with equally objectionable traits? Is not the glorious gift of reason a sufficient compensation? Is not freedom of the mind a glorious enough exchange?

But to those who insist that they "must have something," to them I say:

If you must have a Bible; if you must hoodwink the ignorant; if you must bamboozle the herd; if you must cower the superstitious; if you must have something "divine"; if you must have a "revelation," then by all means let us have something with a little merit in it; something comparable to the intelligence of the day; something representative of the spirit of progress; something actually conducive to the Brotherhood of Man. If you must have "faith in something," have it not in filth.

And in writing your creed and formulating your doctrines, always remember, that *"any system of religion that has anything in it that shocks the mind of a child, cannot be a true system."*

The Creed of Science

By Robert G. Ingersoll

To love justice, to long for the right, to love mercy, to pity the suffering, to assist the weak, to forget wrongs and remember benefits -- to love the truth, to be sincere, to utter honest words, to love liberty, to wage relentless war_ against slavery in all its forms, to love wife and child and friend, to make a happy home, to love the beautiful in art, in nature, to cultivate the mind, to be familiar with the mighty thoughts that genius has expressed, the noble deeds of all the world, to cultivate courage and cheerfulness, to make others happy, to fill life with the splendor of generous acts, the warmth of loving words, to discard error, to destroy prejudice, to receive new truths with gladness, to cultivate hope, to see the calm beyond the storm, the dawn beyond the night, to do the best that can be done and then to be resigned -- this is the religion of reason, the creed of science. This satisfies the heart and brain.

Breinigsville, PA USA
01 September 2010
244747BV00002B/79/A